Organizations and National Culture

Organizations and National Culture

A Comparative Analysis

Monir H. Tayeb

ⓢ SAGE Publications
London • Newbury Park • Beverly Hills • New Delhi

© Monir H. Tayeb 1988

First published 1988

All rights reserved. No part of this publication may be reproduced, stored in a retrieval system, transmitted or utilized in any form or by any means, electronic, mechanical, photocopying, recording or otherwise, without permission in writing from the Publishers.

SAGE Publications Ltd
28 Banner Street
London EC1Y 8QE

SAGE Publications Inc
2111 West Hillcrest Drive
Newbury Park, California 91320

SAGE Publications Inc
275 South Beverly Drive
Beverly Hills, California 90212

SAGE Publications India Pvt Ltd
32, M-Block Market
Greater Kailash – I
New Delhi 110 048

British Library Cataloguing in Publication Data
Tayeb, Monir H.
 Organizations and national culture: a
 comparative analysis.
 1. Organizational behaviour
 I. Title
 302.3'5

ISBN 0–8039–8166–X

Library of Congress catalog card number 88–061483

Typeset by Fakenham Photosetting Ltd, Fakenham, Norfolk
Printed in Great Britain by Billing and Sons Ltd, Worcester

For the Sussex Five

Contents

I INTRODUCTION

1 Introduction — 1

II THEORIES OF ORGANIZATIONS IN NATIONS

2 Universal Theories of Organization — 9

3 Political Economy Theory — 27

4 Cultural Theory — 34

5 Organization and Culture: A Hypothetical Model — 42

III CULTURAL AND ORGANIZATIONAL ASSESSMENT

6 Research Design and Methodology — 49

7 England and India as Social and Cultural Settings for Organizations — 73

8 Cultures, Work-Related Attitudes and Organizational Structure — 107

9 Non-Cultural Influences on Work Attitudes and Organizational Structure — 134

IV CONCLUSIONS

10 Conclusions — 148

References — 161

Index — 173

PART I
INTRODUCTION

1
Introduction

This book presents a cross-national study of cultures and organizations conducted in England and India. The study seeks to enquire whether culture and other societal factors are manifest in work-related attitudes and indeed whether they influence organizational structures and systems. At the same time, it is recognized that non-cultural and contextual factors may also play a significant role in shaping organizations, and their members' attitudes and behaviours.

THE PROBLEM

Previous research has pointed to considerable diversity in organizational structures and management systems. For instance, there are 'tall' and 'slim' organizations, and there are 'flat' and 'fat' organizations (Child, 1984a). There are some which have rigid hierarchies and clear-cut boundaries around jobs and departments, while others resemble shapeless 'tents' pinned down loosely on see-saws (Hedberg et al., 1976). In some organizations departments and employees are coupled loosely, and in some the coupling is tight (Weick, 1976). In some countries there appear to be large variations in organizational forms, in others the range of such variations appears to be restricted (Tayeb, 1979). Many cross-cultural studies have reported similarities between organizations operating in diverse cultural and societal settings (Lammers and Hickson, 1979; Hickson et al., 1981). These similarities were found especially in the relationships between the structural characteristics of organizations on the one hand and their contexts on the other (Hickson et al., 1974). For instance, Negandhi and Prasad (1971) and Negandhi (1985) found that although Indian organizations tended to be more centralized than their North American counterparts, in both countries smaller firms were likely to be more centralized than the larger ones.

Other studies, however, have reported considerable differences between organizations operating in similar task environments but different societies. For instance, Maurice et al. (1980), in a comparison between samples of organizations in France, West Germany and

Britain which had been matched for some contextual factors, found there were differences between them with regard to configuration, work structuring and co-ordination, and qualification and career systems. A study conducted by Ouchi (1981) found there were differences between Japanese and American organizations in areas such as employee–management relationships, communication, the extent of consultation in decision making, and the quality of management of human resources. The question therefore arises as to how such differences and similarities are to be explained.

Many students of organizations have sought to address this question but have not provided particularly convincing answers and explanations. Roberts (1970) likened the endeavours of cross-cultural comparative researchers to that of a group of individuals, each of whom had been looking at different parts of an elephant. This comment can be extended to all those students of organizational structure advocating various perspectives, namely contingency theorists, political economists, and culturalists. Most of them talk about different aspects of one phenomenon. Each group concentrates on one particular 'part' and makes generalizations about the 'whole', or mistakes the part for the whole. This has resulted in a narrow and simplistic view of organizations.

The exclusiveness of various perspectives has at times even led some researchers to adopt research designs which are tailor-made to prove the arguments of only one perspective and are insensitive to others. Thus, as Maurice (1976: 6) points out:

> The rationality of organizations considered a priori universal thus prevents testing national/cultural effects on theoretical and empirical grounds because the concepts, methods, indicators, and operational processes used exclude all references to the social structures to which organizations are definitely related.

In contrast to the claim that different paradigms in organizational analysis are irreconcilable 'world views' (Burrell and Morgan, 1979), the view is taken here that each of these paradigms potentially adds to our total understanding. It is argued that there is a need for a constructive proposition to integrate these differentiated viewpoints and build a comprehensive model to provide a richer and more realistic explanation for organizations as social phenomena. The present study is an attempt to move towards such a model through a cross-national comparative study of organizations. It does not, of course, claim to furnish any final answers to the questions and problems mentioned. The intention, rather, is to explore and clarify the organizationally-relevant role of culture and other societal factors to a somewhat greater extent than has been achieved in most previous research.

This clarification can be both intellectually and practically fruitful because growing internationalism demands that a narrow domestic paradigm be replaced by one that can encompass the diversity of a global perspective (Adler, 1983). As Jelinek et al. (1983: 331) put it:

> To the extent that our ways of looking at things become solidified into commonly accepted paradigms limiting what we pay attention to, new ideas in and of themselves can be valuable. Culture as a root metaphor for organization studies is one such idea, redirecting our attention away from some of the commonly accepted 'important things' (such as structure or technology) and toward the (until now) less-frequently examined elements raised to importance by the new metaphor (such as shared understandings, norms, or values). Especially in conjunction with other approaches, culture may provide the critical tension that can lead to new insights.

The present study also raises certain questions which may stimulate future investigations. For example, in what way and to what extent do cultural and non-cultural factors in and around organizations influence their structures and their members' behaviours? Is centralization, to give a more precise example, determined by the size of the organization under study or the attitudes of its members to people in positions of power and authority? Or is it a combined effect of the two, and/or some other factors, which determines the degree of centralization? What role do education, age, occupation and other 'non-cultural' factors play in employees' work-related values and attitudes? To what extent are the 'non-cultural' factors such as occupation really 'culture-free'?

While the practical utility of the present investigation is likely to be seen most immediately for multinational organizations, in so far as they particularly manifest the growth of global interdependence, its subject is one of wide interest (Smircich, 1983). In multi-cultural societies, such as Britain, the United States, France and West Germany, where immigrants from totally different societies form substantial minorities, the findings of the present and similar research might enlighten the mutual understanding of managers and employees from different cultural backgrounds who work together. For instance, some cultural characteristics, such as attitudes to authority and group-orientation, have obvious implications for relations between management and workers and for acceptable modes of work organizations.

Moreover, the comparisons in this study between organizations operating in an Eastern developing country and those in a Western developed country should address the concerns of people, such as managers and organizational designers, who wish to find a mode of organizing that is not 'advanced' by Western capitalist values but is authentic to their own culture and/or political ideology.

THE AUTHOR'S INTEREST IN THE 'CROSS-NATIONAL STUDY OF ORGANIZATIONS'

I first became familiar with and interested in business organizations when I studied for a degree in Business Studies at Tehran in the late 1960s. I subsequently worked in a government corporation as a middle manager for four years. This experience gave me a deeper insight into the practical issues involved in managerial and organizational processes and structures, such as the parallelism of formal and informal authority structures, policy constraints on the managers' economic decisions, sycophancy, favouritism and corruption. In 1976 I went to Oxford University where, in the pursuit of a Masters research degree in Management Studies, I learned more about Western theories of organization and management and met well-known scholars in the field. I was particularly fascinated by the arguments advanced by the advocates of contingency theory who came mainly from the UK and the US. Briefly, they argued that the success and/or survival of an organization depended on how well it 'matched' its structure to environmental demands. However, having come from a very different country (Iran), I found myself echoing Crozier's objections to contingency assumptions. It seemed to me that British and American contingency theorists had taken their cultural and societal characteristics too much for granted. Crozier's *The Bureaucratic Phenomenon* (1964) shook my naïve fascination with contingency theory. I then met and held discussions with Professor Hofstede, who gave me further encouragement and confidence to challenge contingency arguments on the grounds of their apparent neglect of cultural implications for organizational structure. According to a culturalist view, then, organizational success does not depend on a 'sympathy' between structural and contingency factors. Rather, it depends on a match between an organization's structure and the culturally-derived expectations of its members.

Child's (1972a) article on the 'strategic choices' available to managers was another guide in my path to the understanding of organizations. This suggested that organizational performance can also be achieved by means other than structure–contingency 'fit', such as how well managers are able to choose between various market strategies and operational technologies, the quality of their recruitment policies, and the selection of the location for their operations. The choices made by managers are seen to be based on their evaluation of the situation which is, in turn, influenced by their values, ideologies, preferences and perceptions. The process of 'strategic choice' may therefore limit the extent that environment can determine the organization's structure and behaviour. It certainly implies that the environment–organization relationship is not a simple deterministic one. Moreover, some organizations, especially those operating in protected economies or in the public sector, could afford to survive and flourish at less than an optimum level of performance.

At this stage, I had developed mixed feelings about contingency and cultural perspectives. The arguments put forward by both sides made sense, but somehow they were treated by their respective proponents, with the exception of Child, as if they were mutually exclusive. I decided to test these supposedly 'irreconcilable' viewpoints by conducting a study of Iranian culture and organizations (Tayeb, 1979).

This study confirmed my thoughts about the importance of the contributions made by both the contingency and cultural perspectives to the understanding of organizations. On the one hand, the structures and management styles of the fourteen organizations which participated in the study were compatible with the work-related attitudes and behaviour of a sample of organizational members. The latter were in turn consistent with the cultural traits attributed to Iranian people in general. On the other hand, certain structural characteristics of the participating organizations were, to some extent, consistent with some of their contextual variables. Thus the larger organizations were more 'structured' (specialized and formalized) than the smaller ones; and the public organizations were more bureaucratized than those in the private sector.

The study in Iran led me to the following conclusions:

1 Organizations have to respond to the changes in their environmental conditions if they are to succeed and survive, but this response is also constrained by the cultural characteristics of their members.
2 Some cultures provide organizations with a limited repertoire of variations in the structural forms they can adopt in response to their contextual and contingency demands; in other cultures this repertoire is extensive.
3 Some organizations are protected for economic, social and political reasons and therefore can afford to ignore contingency factors or even misjudge them and yet survive and be successful. In pre-revolutionary Iran this was possible mainly because of the large revenue from oil.
4 In some countries the influence of cultural characteristics may override the influence of contingency factors in shaping their organizations. For instance, mistrust and close direct supervision and control are prominent among Iranian cultural characteristics. In the Iranian study I found that some of the managers who had been educated in American and European universities were aware of

the 'merits' of decentralization of decision making in their organizations as an 'appropriate' response to their changing environment, but they were reluctant to apply such an approach in their own companies. They did not trust subordinates' abilities and intentions to carry out their tasks 'properly'. Indeed, these managers argued that they would stand to benefit if they tightened their control over their employees and made 'important' decisions themselves. Some had chosen to appoint their own close friends and relatives to 'crucial' posts to ensure the 'proper' handling of the organization's tasks.

The study also made me aware of political economic factors surrounding and influencing organizations. For example, in Iran, under the pre-revolution regime, trade unions were not permitted to function. The management could get away with, among other things, any type of control over the workforce without facing any collective resistance. The government purported to be spokesman for employees, especially manual workers, but in effect it geared its industrial relations legislation to the achievement of its own political ends.

During my stay in Britain and exposure to its system of industrial relations, I became aware of the influence that trade unions have over organizational structures and policies, particularly regarding the division of labour. The difference that the absence of strong unions in a country like Iran made to the organization of work and to management policies became very apparent.

When I undertook the Iranian study at Oxford I was inclined to give more weight to culture as a 'determinant' of organizational structure and management systems as compared to contingency and other factors. But when I started the present comparative study at Aston in 1980, I had a more 'open' and balanced view about the various factors which 'influence' organizations: by then my research experience in Iran and my exposure to other studies conducted in various countries, which found other factors to account for organizational structure and behaviour, had made me aware that culture cannot be the 'determinant' of organizations. At most, it is a factor which, along with others, 'influences' organizations. In the process, the term 'culture' also gave way to 'nation', and the study became cross-national as opposed to cross-cultural. This reflects the view that organizations are influenced by other national institutions besides culture (understood as a set of learned shared values and ideas). The term 'nation' not only refers to culture but also to other societal, economic and political institutions which have a bearing on the nature of organizations located in particular countries.

As a consequence of this personal development, three per-

Introduction 7

spectives are considered relevant to the objectives of the present study. The contingency perspective suggests that a 'fit' between an organization's context and its structural arrangements is fundamentally necessary for achieving success and survival. The political economy perspective argues for the determining role of the social and economic structures within which the organization operates. The ideational approach of the culturalist perspective looks to the cultural attitudes and values of organizational members for an explanation of the organization's structure; while the institutional strand of culturalism draws attention to the ways in which institutions mould social values and behaviour, and generate social competences (for example, expertise, or what is regarded socially as 'expertise').

Studies carried out within these three perspectives are reviewed in the next three chapters. While they make valuable contributions to our understanding of organizations, they have been only partially successful in addressing the question of what influences organization and its structure. The reason for their partial success is that they have been confined to the boundaries of their respective frameworks, and hence failed to recognize the contributions of others. This suggests the need for a more complex multi-perspective approach to the study of organizations which would take note of the factors raised by the different perspectives. In a paper written with Child (Child and Tayeb, 1983: 63–4) we pointed out such a need:

> Three major theoretical perspectives currently inform the cross-national study of organizations. Progress in assessing their collective contribution has been held back by a tendency for research within one perspective to devalue or ignore the considerations contained within the other perspectives. One thesis, expressed by the concept of cultured organization, subsumes contingency and political economy factors within a process of culturally-infused action (Sorge, 1983) ... while this thesis draws attention to an important dynamic of organizational development, it appears to exaggerate the autonomy of organizations from the framework of contingency and political economy parameters which set limits to the possibilities open to decision makers. Rather than concentrating on, or claiming primacy for, one theoretical perspective, consideration of all three perspectives is warranted. The cultural, contingency and political economy variables they identify are interactive, although at the same time it may be possible to identify particular influences emanating from each.

PLAN OF THE BOOK

Chapter 2 discusses and evaluates the arguments advanced by scholars who have adopted contingency and other universalistic approaches to the study of organizations. Chapters 3 and 4 review critically the political economy and cultural perspectives' contributions towards the explanations of organizational structures and systems. Chapter 5 proposes a hypothetical model based on the culturalists' assumptions about the influence of culture on organizations. The model, along with other hypotheses of the study, will be put to the test in Chapters 8 and 9.

Part III deals with the comparative research undertaken by the author in England and India to examine the relevance of the three major perspectives for a sample of organizations in the two countries, and to lay the foundations for a multi-perspective model. Chapter 6 describes the design strategy adopted and the methodology employed to collect the data. Chapter 7 discusses the socio-cultural characteristics of English and Indian peoples and presents the findings of the cultural questionnaire surveys which were conducted in the two countries. The chapter also draws together comparisons between the two peoples and on this basis formulates hypotheses about the work-related attitudes likely to be held by English and Indian employees and their consequences for the work organizations in each country.

Chapter 8 sees a transition of the study to specific organizations. It discusses the findings of the work-related attitudes surveys conducted among employees of a sample of carefully matched manufacturing firms in England and India, and the findings of an interview-based investigation which was carried out into the structural and managerial characteristics of the same organizations. Chapter 9 draws attention to the influence of some non-cultural factors on both employees' work-relevant attitudes and the organizational structures and systems.

Part IV concludes the book by interpreting the findings of the various stages of the study and suggesting their likely implications for theory and practice.

A point to note is the way the author has referred to gender in the book. In order to avoid clumsiness and irksome he/she, his/her, the male gender has been employed in some places and the female in others. Reference to any person or role in the text is to female or male without any prejudice.

PART II
THEORIES OF ORGANIZATIONS IN NATIONS

2
Universal Theories of Organization

Researchers have employed a large variety of definitions and measures in an attempt to understand the structural characteristics of organizations (Child, 1972b; Scott, 1975; Mackenzie, 1978; Clegg, 1979; Hunt, 1979; Meyer, 1979; Cummings, 1982). For instance, Child (1972b: 92) defined organizational structure as 'the formal allocation of work roles and the administrative mechanism to control and integrate work activities including those which cross formal organizational boundaries'. Clegg (1979: 122) argued that organization structure 'can be conceived in terms of the selectivity rules which can be analytically constructed as an explanation of its social action and practice'.

There seems to be some agreement that the main dimensions of structure are centralization, formalization, and complexity, that is, number of hierarchical levels, number of functions, departments or jobs, number of operating sites, and the level of specialist expertise (Pugh et al., 1968). Administrative intensity (ratio of administrative personnel to total or production personnel) has also been considered an important aspect of organizational structure (Ford and Slocum, 1977).

Writers who have sought to establish the predictors of the shapes and forms of organizational structure can be grouped into three broad categories: the universalists, the political economists and the culturalists. This chapter discusses the arguments of the first category, and the following two chapters deal with the others.

CONTINGENCY THEORY

For the first half of this century, management and organization theorists tended to ignore the environment in which organizations operated and argued for a universalistic 'one best way' of organizing work organizations and prescribed bureaucracy as the rational and efficient model of organizations (Taylor, 1911; Urwick, 1943; Brown, 1945; Mooney, 1947; Weber, 1947; Fayol, 1949; Brech, 1953).

Later generations of theorists challenged their predecessors on human relations grounds (Roethlisberger, 1944; Mayo, 1945; McGregor, 1960), but still implied that there was a 'one best way' of organizing activities, with an emphasis on human beings' needs and abilities which, according to this new school, had been overlooked by the classical theorists.

The contingency approach was developed as a challenge to the universal single pattern of structure or organizations advocated by both classical and human relations schools. The primary criticisms made by contingency writers concerned the alleged inability of bureaucracies to adapt to the changes in the environment.

The premises of the contingency perspective are based on the argument that the survival of an organization depends upon its efficient and effective (optimum) performance. This optimum performance, in turn, can be achieved if the organization responds and adapts to its environmental demands 'appropriately'. The appropriate response is crystallized in a 'match' or 'fit' between structural characteristics and contextual and other environmental variables (Lawrence and Lorsch, 1967). For example, an increase in the number of employees should be accompanied by an increase in specialization, or an increase in environmental uncertainty should be 'matched' by an increase in decentralization, if the organization is to achieve a 'high' level of performance.

These assumptions are open to question on a number of grounds. First, the concept of 'high' performance, and indeed, performance itself, is a problematic one. If performance is defined and measured in terms of achievement of goals, whose goals are to be achieved? Managers? Shopfloor workers? Shareholders? Government? Public at large? A certain level of performance can be interpreted as 'high' or 'low' depending on how one answers these questions.

Secondly, the level of performance of an organization is achieved not in a vacuum but under certain conditions which are more often than not constraints, and of which inadequate structural arrangements are but one. Besides, how does one isolate and assess the impact of each of the various factors, including the structural 'match', on performance level?

Thirdly, high performance, whatever that might be, can also be achieved by means other than adjustment and rearrangement of the organizational structure, such as choosing more appropriate overall policies and strategies (Child, 1972a), setting more feasible and realistic objectives, and setting up adequate training courses for the employees to equip themselves with the necessary knowledge and skills to meet the challenges of the world outside.

Fourthly, performance need not always be evaluated against financial and other economic criteria, as is implied by the arguments advanced by the researchers advocating the contingency perspective. Performance can also be measured in terms of social, political and humanitarian criteria. It is, therefore, quite possible for an organization's peformance to be considered poor in economic terms but high in non-economic terms.

Fifthly, the survival of organizations does not necessarily depend upon high and optimum performance. Monopolies, nationalized firms and companies operating in heavily protected industries, for instance, can afford to be sub-optimal.

As a consequence of the contingency perspective, considerable research has been directed toward isolating factors upon which an organization's structure may be contingent. The vast majority of these studies have focused on technology, size, environmental uncertainty, industry, strategy and dependence. The following sections deal with these factors.

Technology

Perrow (1967) defined technology as the actions an individual takes upon an object so as to bring about a change in that object. Marsh and Mannari (1981) defined it as the means by which an organization's outputs are created. Whatever definitions various researchers have given, the main concern, as Thompson and Bates (1957) state, has been those sets of person–machine activities that together produce a desired good.

Woodward's (1958) research was a seminal study into the impact of technology on organizational structure. In her research in a hundred firms engaged in widely diverse lines of business, she found that when the firms were grouped according to their techniques of production and complexity of their production systems, the more successful companies in each of these groupings employed similar management practices. In general, firms at the extremes of technological complexity (unit and continuous process) tended towards 'organic' management styles and structures, whereas those at the centre were more 'mechanistic'. The research led her to conclude that the criterion of the appropriateness of organizational structure must be the extent to which it furthers the objectives of the firm.

Woodward's conclusions are less than reliable on at least two grounds. First, her performance measures are open to question. She does not give any information on the level of performance of the firms concerned apart from saying that they were classified into three broad categories of average, below average and above average. Her performance criteria, moreover, are (a) subjective, such as 'quality and attitudes of management': (b) vague, such as rate of development (she does not elaborate what it is and how she has assessed it): and (c) in the case of objective criteria, such as profitability and market standing, it is not clear from her report whether these have been considered for each firm for the financial year in which the study was conducted or over a period of years. If the former is the case, then the firms' growth and ability to expand are overlooked in the evaluation of their performance.

Secondly, her technology scale also suffers from limitations. The scale consists of five increasingly advanced and complex types of technology. A major limitation, as Marsh and Mannari point out, lies in the assumption that a single dominant type of technology is used in each firm. Among their fifty Japanese factories, 'although twenty-seven used only one of the five types of technology, thirteen used two types, five used three types, four used four types, and one used all five types simultaneously' (Marsh and Mannari, 1981: 37). Khandwalla (1974: 81) found that 'a firm manufacturing telephone switching equipment to customer specification is using custom technology in the design of the equipment, but mass produces the parts and components going to the assembly'.

Many other researchers (Perrow, 1967; Harvey, 1968; Hage and Aiken, 1969; Zwerman, 1970; Van de Ven and Delbecq, 1974; Van de Ven et al., 1974; Blau et al., 1976) followed Woodward and argued for the 'imperatives' of technology and recommended an appropriate 'fit' between structural arrangements and production technology as the means to ensure high performance.

The works of Woodward and her followers had a major impact on organizational theory and provoked and stimulated a series of fruitful intellectual debates and empirical investigations. However, the 'technological imperative' thesis that they proposed suffers from certain drawbacks. First, the thesis is an unjustified sweeping generalization. Although many studies supported the 'fit' between technology and structure as the means to achieve success, no number of successful firms whose structures fit the demands of their production technology, to paraphrase Popper (Popper, 1979), justifies the assumption that all successful firms have a structure which fits the requirements of their technology. As it turned out, there were many other studies which did not support Woodward and her followers (see, for example, Mohr, 1971; Mahoney and Frost, 1974; Donaldson, 1976). In fact, Woodward (1970) herself toned down the technological implications argument contained in her 1958 and 1965 publications. Reeves and Woodward (1970) remarked that it was actually the nature of the interdependency created by technology and methods of organizational control, rather than technology per se, that affects organizational structure.

Secondly, if one can accept for a moment the argument that there should be a fit between technology and structure as a means to achieve high performance, there is more than one way to achieve this fit. According to modern socio-technical theory the aims should be to achieve joint optimization on technology and social/organizational variables, which gives rise to the possibility of more than one structural arrangement (Trist, 1981).

Thirdly, the advocates of the 'technological imperative' thesis overemphasize the role of technology as the determinant of organizational structure, and, by doing so, neglect other factors in and around the organization. Perrow (1977: 97), a former supporter of 'technological imperatives', has reconsidered his position and points out:

> I once believed that if organizations had a better fit between their technology and their structure they would be more efficient and thus more profitable. In a study of a number of firms in various industries I learned what should have been obvious to me at the outset: if the Ys are growth and profitability, the Xs should not be the fit between technology and structure but such variables as market position, industry profitability and growth, brand identification, collusion, bribery, and falsification of accounting records. These related directly to what pose as profitability and growth.

Fourthly, technology, far from being a given and 'imperative' imposed on the organization's managers, can be a 'tool in their hands' to exert control over the employees as well as the production design, leading ultimately to higher productivity (Friedman, 1977a; Child and Tayeb, 1983).

However, the contradictory and confusing findings of the studies carried out to investigate the impact of technology on organizational structure may be to some extent due to inadequacies and inconsistencies in their design and methodologies (Reimann and Inzerilli, 1979). Most of these works concerned technology only and overlooked its implications in conjunction with other factors, such as size, dependence and environmental uncertainty, which may have equally significant bearing on the organization. Moreover, the findings of most of these studies are not comparable because they have employed different measurements (see, for instance, Perrow, 1967; Khandwalla, 1974; Marsh and Mannari, 1981). As Ford and Slocum (1977) point out, many studies that found weak relationships between technology and structure focused exclusively on operations technology (Hickson et al., 1969; Child and Mansfield, 1972), even though these same writers argued that organizations may employ more than one type of technology.

One cannot, therefore, argue strongly or convincingly for or against the role of technology as a determinant of organizational structure. It is argued, however, that although technology may not have an overriding influence on structure, it is nonetheless an important factor, and no serious investigation into organizations and their structural predictors can afford to overlook it. The significance of technology is particularly pronounced because of, for instance, the built-in bias in its design to further capitalistic or socialistic objectives; or the way the so-called new technology can be employed by managers to up-grade and down-grade various jobs, or indeed even create or abolish jobs (Child, 1984a).

Size

Size has attracted a good deal of attention as a predictor of organizational structure. There is no consensus as to how size should be measured, but the most widely accepted definition of an organization's size is the number of its employees.

Many researchers have found a strong relationship between size and organizational structure. Child (1972b), for instance, found that size was an important predictor of the degree of decentralization of decision making. Although the results of a considerable number of studies supported the importance of size as a determinant of organizational structure (Hickson et al., 1969; Inkson et al., 1970; Blau and Schoenherr, 1971; Hinings and Lee, 1971; Child and Mansfield, 1972; Osborn and Hunt, 1974; Ayuobi, 1975; Yassai-Ardekani, 1979; Grinyer and Yassai-Ardekani, 1980), there were others which did not do so (Hall et al., 1967; Mayhew et al., 1972; Blau et al., 1976; Evers et al., 1976; Marsh and Mannari, 1981). Thompson (1967), for example, argued against the impact of size on structure, and stated that if the workflow or task is simple, for example, copper mining, then an increase in scale could be managed without a more elaborate or complex managerial superstructure.

Aldrich (1972: 34) argued that there were several alternative and equally plausible paths relating size, technology and structure. One showed technology to determine structure, which in turn determined size:

> The development of an organization proceeds from its initial founding and capitalization in response to market opportunities, through its design based on copying and modifying an existing technology, on to the design of the organization's structure, and finally to the employment of a workforce to staff the nearly completed organization... Technology is causally superior to the size of the workforce ... and is also causally superior to organization structure.

A problem with the studies which focused on size, and indeed also those which concerned other contextual factors, is that they failed to explain why technology, size etc., led to a particular structure, and what were the processes involved. The interrelationships between size and other factors and their combined impact on structure have not been sufficiently explored. Also, in many of the studies size has been measured in different and inconsistent ways, leading to conflicting conclusions (Kimberly, 1976).

Size, however, is a major aspect or dimension of an organizational anatomy and there is more to learn about its implications for organizations. For example, is an increase in size per se important or is it the increase in its quality (in terms of know-how) that matters? How do different cultures cope with an increase in size? Does a larger size lead to a greater decentralization in all organizations in all cultures?

Environment

Environment is one of the most widely discussed concepts, and it has been defined in many ways. Pennings (1975: 393–4) gives a useful broad definition which encompasses relevant factors that surround organizations:

> Environment is the organization's source of inputs and sink of outputs; that is, the set of persons, groups, and organizations with which the focal organization has exchange relations.

Osborn and Hunt (1974: 231–2) grouped the various broad elements in and around organizations into three categories: 'macro', 'aggregate', and 'task' environments:

> The macro environment is the general cultural context of a specified geographical area and contains those factors recognized to have important influences on organizational characteristics and outputs ... The aggregate environment consists of the associations, interest groups, and constituencies operating within a given macro environment ... Typically, the task environment is defined as that portion of the total setting which is relevant for goal setting and goal attainment. (Dill, 1958; Thorelli, 1967)

Of these, the task environment has attracted the attention of most writers on environment–structure relationships. Many of these researchers emphasize that organizations must adapt to their environment if they are to retain and/or increase their effectiveness. Much of the theoretical and empirical work on this issue has focused on uncertainty and unpredictability.

Burns and Stalker (1961) noted that successful firms in a stable environment tended to have a 'mechanistic' or highly bureaucratic structure and process, while successful firms in a changing and uncertain environment tended to have an 'organic' or flexible structure with low centralization and low formalization. It must be pointed out that Burns and Stalker had only one example of an organic unit (and it was only the R & D department of a firm, not the firm as a whole). This takes us to the question of intra-organization structural variations as proposed by Lawrence and Lorsch (1967).

They operationalized environmental uncertainty by measuring the clarity of information, the degree to which cause–effect relationships are known, and the time span of definitive feedback. They then characterized an organization's environment as diverse if a wide range of uncertainty existed among its different parts, and homogeneous if the range was narrow. Studying a sample of six firms from three industries, they found that in successful organizations, each sub-unit met the demands of its own environment. In diverse environments, sub-units were more differentiated than those in the homogeneous environments, and more efforts were required to integrate the differentiated sub-units in the diverse environments than in the homogeneous ones. Differentiation, in this case, refers not only to differences in formal structure, but also to the differences in the cognitive and emotional orientations of the members of the sub-units.

Cohen et al. (1972) proposed a 'garbage can' model for organizations operating under the conditions of uncertainty, where technology is unclear and goals are ambiguous; while Hedberg et al. (1976) advised the residents of changing environments to take a 'tent' and 'camp on see-saws' in order to achieve and maintain the required flexibility, creativity, immediacy and initiative. Weick (1976) prescribed 'loosely coupled' systems for organizations as an appropriate response to changing environments.

The writers whose studies were described in this section treated environmental uncertainty as if the environment could per se be 'uncertain'. Duncan (1971a, 1971b, 1972) was among the first to direct attention to 'perceived uncertainty', and provided a systematic conceptualization and empirical analysis of the dimensions of environment that lead to different degrees of perceived uncertainty. He suggested that perceived environmental uncertainty in a decision-making situation is determined by two dimensions: the simple–complex dimension (number of factors considered in decision making and their degree of similarity) and the static–dynamic dimension (the degree to which these factors change). From a study of managers in twenty-two decision units, Duncan concluded that the static–dynamic dimension was a more important determinant of perceived uncertainly than the simple–complex dimension. He also identified the types of structural modifications that decision units implemented under uncertainty and the relationships between these adaptation processes and organizational effectiveness.

Universal theories of organization 17

In the 1970s a new stream of thought was developed which studied organizations as species in relation to their environments. Exponents of this approach proposed a 'natural selection' or 'population ecology' model (Aldrich and Pfeffer, 1976). This model, developing the strongest argument for an environmental perspective, applies at the population level of organizations rather than at the level of single units. Environment differentially selects organizations for survival on the basis of the fit between organizational structure (and activities) and environmental characteristics (Buckley, 1967; Campbell, 1969; Aldrich, 1971; Hannan and Freeman, 1974). The process of organizational change, while controlled by the environment, does not necessarily involve progress to more complex or higher forms of social organizations, or better organizations. The process of natural selection means the social organizations are moving towards a better 'fit' with the environment, nothing more (Aldrich and Pfeffer, 1976; Aldrich, 1979; McKelvey and Aldrich, 1983).

The writers who advocate 'environmental determinism' can be criticized on at least one major ground. They appear to assume that the organization–environment relationship is a one-way flow of 'demand' and 'command' from the environment to which the organization has to adapt passively by way of making the necessary structural arrangements and modifications, if it is to be successful and, indeed, to survive. These researchers have clearly ignored the organization's members, especially managers, who, albeit subject to constraints, have power and resources to influence, change and even create their own environments as they see fit (Cyert and March, 1963; Thompson, 1967; Weick, 1969). It is astonishing that these researchers, who are almost all from Western societies with an established philosophy of faith in human's ability to conquer his or her environment, do not recognize the same ability in organizations and their members.

There are some writers who have recognized the importance of the role of managers in managing their organizations and their environments. In this conjunction, Child (1972a) introduced the notion of 'strategic choice' which is exercised by the organizational elite and other members of the 'dominant coalition'. This view of the determinants of organizational activities is introduced to account for how decisions are actually made, given that environment, technology and size are not totally responsible for organizational change or stability. Anderson and Paine (1975) and Bobbit and Ford (1980) have supported Child and argued that decision makers' choice is a determinant of organizational structure.

Exponents of the 'resource dependence' model argue along similar lines. The model proceeds from the proposition that organizations are not able to generate internally either all the resources or functions required to maintain themselves, and therefore organizations must enter into transactions and relations with elements in the environment that can supply the required resources and services. Administrators, who must ensure a continued supply of resources to maintain satisfaction of their organization's members, owners, and other powerful groups in their environment (White, 1974), manage their environments as well as their organizations. The resource dependence model portrays organizations as active, and capable of changing as well as responding to the environment. The model calls attention to the importance of environmental contingencies and constraints while at the same time leaving room for the operation of strategic choice on the part of the organizational members as they manoeuvre through known and unknown contexts (Pfeffer, 1972; Jacob, 1974; Pfeffer and Salancik, 1974, 1978).

Industry

Industry is a significant variable because of the implications for organizations of such factors as the age of the industry, the organization's standing within it in terms of market share and power, competition, change, and governmental economic and industrial policies and priorities. For instance, firms engaged in the electronics industry face fierce competition and a rapidly changing climate compared to the brewery industry. This instability is made even greater in some Western countries, such as Britain, by their governments' 'open door' policies. In contrast, in a country like India, with highly protective industrial policies, there is relatively little competition in the market confronting the electronics firms. These firms, however, face a dilemma of a different kind. Because the electronics industry is capital intensive, and because the government's economic priority is to create employment for millions of jobless people, there is a restriction on the total production and expansion of the firms engaged in this industry.

Spender (1980), in a study of foundry, dairy, and fork-lift truck rental industries, argued that there is an industry-specific 'recipe' which bears most heavily on organizational strategy-makers and influences their policies, objectives and judgements.

Hrebiniak and Snow (1980) sought to examine whether industry was an important variable for the kind of uncertainty perceived by top managers and for the patterns of organizational structure and influence. Their study showed that perceptions of environmental uncertainty, interorganizational influence, and the degree of structural decentralization varied by industry. Their data also indicated that structural responses to environmental uncertainty were affected by industry, suggesting that the structure–contingency model was comprised of 'models', depending on organizational domain or setting.

Strategy

The area of structure–strategy–environment has also received considerable attention within the contingency framework. The concept of organizational strategy was advanced by the Harvard Business School in the late 1950s to embrace the major decisions that serve to match organizational resources with environmental opportunities and constraints (Andrews, 1960; Chandler, 1962). The major systematic insights into the relationships between environment, strategy and structure stem from Chandler's historical studies. He concentrated on the changing strategies of seventy-five large American corporations and analysed their grouping efforts to devise new organizational structures to pursue these strategies more effectively.

Following Chandler, Scott (1970) developed a paradigm of corporate development that views the firm as moving through successive stages as its product–market relationship becomes more elaborate. In this 'stage model' the firm is seen as growing from a 'one-man show' to a functionally-organized structure, and then, as it develops multiple product lines, to a product–division structure.

Miles and Snow (1978) developed a model of organizational adaptation and argued that every organization chooses its own target market and develops its own set of products or services, and these domain decisions will then be supported by appropriate decisions concerning the organization's technology, structure, and processes. Management is relatively free to choose among alternative forms of each of these major organizational features. They identified four broad categories of such forms: 'defenders', 'prospectors', 'analysers', and 'reactors', each of which has its own strategy in its interactions with the environment.

Rumelt (1986), basing his analysis on the data from more than 200 American companies, found a positive relationship between performance on the one hand, and a fit between strategy and organizational structure on the other. However, he also suggested that structure follows fashion.

Miller et al. (1982) studied a sample of thirty-three business firms in Canada and attempted to establish whether there was any relationship between the personality of the top executives and their strategy-making behaviour, and whether this in turn had any implications for structure and environment. The locus of control of top executives was a personality characteristic that they saw held much promise in explaining strategy-making behaviour. Confident, aggressive, and active chief executives, they argued, tend to undertake more innovative, risky and proactive strategies; executives who are more given to feelings of helplessness and passivity are more conservative, reactionary and risk averse, and this in turn has repercussions on the dimensions of environment and structure.

Strategy, although a significant factor, has not been sufficiently studied within a cross-national comparative framework to examine whether its influence on structure is as universally great as its advocates believe. Clearly further research is needed in this area.

Findings of the Aston Programme

Researchers involved in the Aston Programme (Pugh et al., 1968) attributed the structural characteristics of organizations to certain variables in their context. Their first major study covered forty-six organizations in Birmingham, England. They identified and developed scales for five structural dimensions. These were centralization, specialization, formalization, standardization and configuration. Contextual variables which the Aston researchers considered as being predictors of the state of the structural dimensions were origin and history, ownership and control, location and resources, dependence on parent organization, size, technology and charter. Child, in his National Study (1972b) in which he replicated the Aston Programme in eighty-two organizations throughout Britain, argued that the status of the focal organization, that is whether it is an independent company, a parent company, a subsidiary, a division, a department or a production unit, has significant implications for its structure, especially the degree of centralization of decision making.

Later generations of writers extended the concept of 'dependence' on parent company to include dependence on other organizations, such as suppliers and customers. This dependence, they argued, affects the focal organization's autonomy and dispersion of decision making (McMillan et al., 1973; Horvath et al., 1976). Hickson et al. (1969) went on further to argue that such dependence has similar implications for organizations in all countries.

Subsequent research and replications of the Programme refuted many of the earlier findings. The Programme was also criticized on methodological grounds (Aldrich, 1972; Child, 1972b, 1973; Mansfield, 1973; Pennings, 1973; Khandwalla, 1974; Brossard and Maurice, 1976; Ford, 1977; Kmetz, 1978; Grinyer and Yassai-Ardekani, 1980). However, the Programme remains a major attempt to provide an organizational taxonomy and a model for understanding the organization's relationships with its immediate context.

The culture-free thesis

One of the most controversial arguments for the determining role of contextual and other contingency variables in the organizational structure was put forward by Hickson et al. (1974) who advocated a universal 'culture-free' thesis. The thrust of their argument is that the relationship between organizational characteristics and their contextual variables is stable across societies:

> ... [Our] hypothesis rests on the theory that there are imperatives, or 'causal' relationships, from the resources of 'customers', of employees, of materials and finance, etc., and of operating technology, to its structure, which take effect whatever the surrounding social differences ... Whether the culture is Asian or European or North American, a large organization with many employees improve efficiency by specializing their activities but also by increasing controlling and coordinating specialities. (Hickson et al., 1974: 63–4)

Haire et al.'s (1966) well known study also led them to advocate universalism in 'managerial thinking' across cultures. They studied attitudes, perceived needs and need satisfaction of a sample of about 3,600 managers from fourteen countries, the majority of whom were attending management training courses at the time and had been selected by the researchers 'impressionistically and sometimes opportunistically' (pp. 6–7). The researchers noted that only 25 percent of the observed differences among the participants were associated with their national differences, and the similarities among these managers were far more numerous than their differences.

Two points should be borne in mind with respect to the culture-free thesis and the universalism assumed on the basis of these two, and similar, studies. First, some of the studies carried out within this framework suffer from methodological inadequacies. Take Haire et al.'s work. The managers whose attitudes were studied were attending management training courses at the time the research was carried out. This means they were subject to a similar flow of instructions about modern management practices and theories which could well have influenced their responses to the questionnaire they completed. Moreover, Haire et al. neither studied the structural characteristics of the organizations which were managed by these managers, nor surveyed the attitudes of their subordinates to examine how they perceived their managers ran the organization. To agree with statements favouring, say, a participative management style is one thing; actually to behave like a participative manager is another.

Secondly, the purpose of studies such as Hickson et al.'s is to test the stability of relationships between organizational structure and its environmental variables, rather than to examine their underlying rationale (Maurice, 1976). They look for similarities rather than differences in organizations operating in different countries.

> Thus, when certain formal characteristics of organization structures (centralization, formalization, specialization, etc.) are related to such contextual variables as size and technology, it is important to realize that these studies are based on concepts and indicators that by nature are universal – thereby precluding any testing of the impact of national or cultural variables in which such studies express interest. (Maurice, 1976: 5–6)

CONTINGENCY THEORY – AN OVERALL VIEW

The main strength of the contingency approach lies in its valuable contribution to the understanding of organizations, by pointing out the importance of the interaction between the organizations and their environment and the role that this interaction plays in shaping their structure and processes. This theory was the first approach to organization theory to state the now accepted view that there is no 'one best way' of managing work organizations, and that a degree of choice was available to managers as to how to manage their organizations, given certain environmental conditions.

The contingency theory, however, suffers from a number of drawbacks which are more or less attributable to all the works carried out within its framework. One problem with this approach lies in the inconsistency in its arguments and the findings of the studies conducted within its framework. For instance, the pioneers of the school started by condemning the 'universalism' of the classical and human relations theorists, and by advocating an 'it all depends' thesis. They ended up, however, by prescribing a limited number of universal structural forms and management styles depending on, for example, technological requirements and environmental uncertainty.

Secondly, as was discussed earlier, there are also contradictions between the findings of the various studies carried out on organizational structure. These contradictions may have something to do with the way these studies were carried out within the contingency framework rather than the framework itself. For instance, Child (1972b) pointed out that differences in the units of analysis may cause differences in the research results. Observing discrepancies between his results and those of Pugh et al.'s (1968) and Hinings and Lee's (1971), he suggested that these differences might be due to the heterogeneity in the status of the Aston sample.

Thirdly, as Schoonhoven (1981: 349–50) comments, the contingency theory suffers from a lack of clarity and theoretical ambiguity:

> Statements from contingency theorists and researchers suggest that a particular structure should be 'appropriate for' a given environment (Thompson, 1967), that organizations are more successful when their

structures 'conform' to their technologies (Woodward, 1965: 69–71), that an organization's internal states and processes should be 'consistent with' external demands (Lawrence and Lorsch, 1967), that organizations should attempt to maximize 'congruence' between technology and their structure and adapt their structure to 'fit' their technology (Perrow, 1970: 80), that technology and structure need to be properly 'aligned' (Khandwalla, 1974: 97), that a 'coalignment' should exist between environment and structure (Lawrence, 1975), and that communication structures should 'match' the nature of the task (Tushman, 1978). Contingency theory currently requires greater precision than is provided by these richly suggestive but ambiguous statements.

Fourthly, the contingency theorists' discussion of the way environmental factors affect organizational structure is sometimes superficial and lacks a deep analysis of their implications. For instance, they argue for the importance of the economic market surrounding the organization, but they fail to investigate the market–organization relationships in terms of the power and dominance that the organization might enjoy in the market vis-à-vis its customers, its suppliers and its labour force (Child and Tayeb, 1983). What Child (1984a) calls the 'political contingency' school has begun to investigate this issue.

Fifthly, the studies conducted within the framework suffer from methodological inadequacies. They have, for instance, investigated the impact of contextual variables on organizational structure not in relation to each other and in a collective manner, but one by one across two or more organizations. A research design such as this neglects the impact of other factors and their combined effects, and by-passes the tension created in particular by the conflicting demands imposed by them. For instance, what happens if an organization's technology demands a highly decentralized and flexible structure but its stable economic market and small size demand the opposite? Studies that have addressed this and similar questions are few and far between.

This leads to a sixth problem. Contextual variables may not only have different and conflicting implications for the organization; they may also affect different parts of the organization. For instance, a change in the production technology from a routine and simple one to a more complex and non-routine technology may affect the production plant, but a change in the export policies may have implications for the marketing department. How is one to know which variable to what degree has affected which part(s) of the organization? Contingency theorists have done little to adequately investigate such matters.

Seventhly, although later advocates of the contingency approach, following Child (1972a), recognized the role of managers' perceptions and preferences in their dealings with environment, they assumed a universal pattern of perceptions and preferences under similar circumstances across cultural boundaries. This assumption manifests itself explicitly in the 'culture-free' thesis. This denial of the influence of culture on the behaviour of employees and the structure of their organization is a major drawback of the contingency theory.

THEORIES OF EXCELLENCE

Theories of excellence are among the latest trends in the study of organization. They were built on the success stories reported by Ouchi (1981) and Peters and Waterman (1982), and further expanded in publications such as *The One Minute Manager* (Blanchard and Johnson, 1982), and *Megatrends* (Naisbitt, 1982). These books, which in their own way made history by putting management books on the top of the bestselling lists, have largely been ignored by academics. However, as Soeters (1986) points out, the writers of these books do offer significant contributions to the field of organization theory.

The thrust of the arguments put forward by these writers is that the economic success of an organization depends ultimately on the kind of culture and value systems it has. Ouchi's *Theory Z* rests on the trinity of trust, subtlety and intimacy. Z organizations, a cross breed of Japanese-style and American-style organizations, benefit from the best of both worlds. They are characterized by (a) a holistic concern for people; (b) long-term, often life-time employment; (c) non-specialized career paths, employees wandering around functions and offices; (d) use of formal control mechanisms together with non-quantitative, subtle, subjective judgement; (e) a 'clannish' participative decision-making structure with the ultimate responsibility for decisions lying in the hands of one person; and (f) long-term relationships with high trust and common objectives.

Theory Z was the launching pad for Peters and Waterman's *In Search of Excellence*. After a series of preliminary interviews, the authors chose a sample of forty-three American companies for further detailed studies. The criterion for inclusion in the sample was economic success, reflected in long-term productivity over a period of twenty years, and measured using six indicators such as asset and equity growth, average return on total capital, and ratio of market to book value. The study identified eight principles which characterized the 'excellent' companies:

1 A bias for action: a preference for doing something – anything – rather than sending a question through cycles of analyses and committee reports.

2 Staying close to customer – learning his or her preferences and catering to them.
3 Autonomy and entrepreneurship – breaking the corporation into small companies and encouraging them to think independently and competitively.
4 Productivity through people – creating in all employees the awareness that their best efforts are essential and that they will share in the rewards of the company's success.
5 Hands-on, value driven – insisting that executives keep in touch with the firm's essential business.
6 Stick to the knitting – remaining with the business the company knows best.
7 Simple form, lean staff – few administrative layers, few people at the upper levels.
8 Simultaneous loose–tight properties – fostering a climate where there is dedication to the central values of the company combined with tolerance for all employees who accept those values.

Peters and Waterman imply that the companies which followed all or most of these principles of excellence, regardless of the environments within which they operated, were economically successful.

Their findings, however, should be considered with extreme caution for a variety of reasons. First, the measures on the basis of which the authors chose their 'excellent' companies reflected growth and financial success only, and not the companies' success in achieving and maintaining high standards of employee morale and well-being. As Mitchell (1985) demonstrates, the majority of these firms are not the best companies to work for. Soeters (1986) reports that recently in the United States leaflets were sold carrying the message 'I would rather be dead than excellent' (see also Ray, 1986).

Secondly, the sampling procedures are not quite clear. The authors chose forty-three companies for inclusion in the study because they were at the top of their industry in at least four of the six measures of excellence, but the book refers explicitly to only fourteen of these companies. The reason these fourteen firms were selected remains unclear. This, as Soeters (1986) points out, renders the research less than methodologically sound.

Thirdly, environmental factors, such as technology and market and the ability of the firms to cope with these, have been excluded from the authors' analyses. By 1984, two years after the publication of *In Seach of Excellence*, at least fourteen of the forty-three companies studied were no longer 'excellent' because they had failed to adapt to fundamental changes in their markets. For instance, according to *Business Weekly* (5 November 1984), a computer manufacturing firm had to fold its home computer business after millions of dollars of loss. Its engineers, accustomed to industrial customers, lacked expertise in consumer markets. The company cut prices to create demand for its home computer, but this tactic, borrowed from its industrial-chip markets, failed to generate a lasting interest. Another firm was so out of touch with its market that it failed to realize its customers were losing interest in video-game players and were switching to home computers.

Fourthly, like many American writers, Peters and Waterman's prescription for success is anchored in American culture and may not necessarily work elsewhere. Besides, as Smith and Peterson (1988) point out, they confound together 'what is to be done and how it is to be done'. The 'what' part of their prescription is of general and etic nature; whereas the 'how' part of it is of a more specific and emic nature. Organizations may indeed have to have 'a bias for action', but not all may achieve this by 'managing by walking about'. This aspect may well be different from culture to culture or even organization to organization (Smith and Tayeb, 1988).

3
Political Economy Theory

There are some researchers who do not consider themselves followers of the contingency theory, but they argue all the same for the significant influences of broad environmental factors, such as the degree and process of industrialization (Harbison and Myers, 1959; Dore, 1973), macro-economic structure (Child, 1980, 1984b), and labour market (Freidman, 1977a), on organizational structure and management practices. These researchers play down the role of national culture, and assume a far-reaching role for political and economic supra-structures which are argued to suppress local differences. The folowing sections will discuss these propositions in detail.

THE LOGIC OF INDUSTRIALIZATION

This thesis basically argues that there is a central logic to industrialization which derives from the imperatives of machine technology and economic development. Industrialization brings about certain changes in the fabric of organizations, particularly in their size and complexity. These changes in turn are seen as necessitating certain developments in organization structuring: greater specialization, reliance upon rules and decentralization. Management becomes more 'professionalized' and authority relationships tend to shift from autocratic to formalized and more participative modes. The logic of industrialization prevails whatever the cultural setting, although cultural factors can impinge on the process and may slow it down (Harbison and Myers, 1959).

Dore (1973) suggested a further aspect to the logic of industrialization thesis by arguing that the way a country comes to industrialization can have a lasting effect on the kind of industrial society it becomes. He compared development of labour movements and industrial relations and their bearing on management policies and practices in Japan with those in Britain since the beginning of industrialization in the two countries. In Britain, industrialization was a long drawn-out process which started in the mid-eighteenth century and spread over a period of 200 years. In Japan it started in the first quarter of the twentieth century, and the country 'jumped' from a feudal form of corporatism to a modern form of enterprise without ever experiencing either the sturdy independence or the callous indifference to one's neighbour of a thorough-going *laissez-faire* market economy. On the basis of this study, Dore made some speculations about the effect of what he called the 'late development syndrome' on organization and management practices:

> ... The later the industrialization, the bigger the organizational leap, the more likely industry is to begin with rationalized bureaucratic forms of organization, and the more the right of trade unions and workers will be stressed. Corporations in the contemporary late starters, sending their personnel officers to business schools in Europe and America, begin with industrialization under the influence of human relations theories and 'Y' theories, and theories about the virtues of consultation with workplace representatives. (Dore, 1973: 416)

Dore, however, does not provide any evidence that the Japanese managers are actually influenced by American- and European-based modern Y-type theories of management. On the contrary, judging by the findings of more recent studies of Japanese organizations (De Bettignies, 1973; Ouchi, 1981; Smith, 1984), Japanese managers have developed their own brand of management style quite distinct from that which Dore assumes.

SOCIO-ECONOMIC SYSTEM

Relatively few studies have been carried out to examine the influence of the two major forms of the economic system of production, namely capitalism and socialism, of organization structure. The two systems appear to stand in sharp ideological and institutional contrast. As Lane (1977: 173) states:

> State ownership of the means of production, the dominance of working-class values and the absence of an antagonistic ascendant class in state socialist society ensures its basic character as a workers' state. Its chief forms of production are socialist. Western capitalist societies have a quite different basis and dynamic: they are characterized by social classes which have rights over disposal of property and of income from property; the capital market and the making of profit in the context of a more or less regulated economy are essential dynamics of the system.

The debate, however, continues as to whether the development of both capitalist and socialist societies is eroding the differences between them, and whether it would be more accurate to distinguish several variants of capitalism and socialism. Nevertheless, as Child and Tayeb (1983) put it, as long as each system rests upon intrinsically different functions it is to be expected that their organized units will reflect the different basis and dynamic of each system.

Child and Tayeb (1983) and Child (1984b) discussed the likely implications of these differences for organizational objectives and relations, ideology, planning, resource allocation and control, and organizational hierarchies. In principle, the objectives of the capitalist economic organization are directed towards profit maximization and the strategies for attaining these are formulated in the light of market conditions governing the value secured for products when these are exchanged. In contrast, the objectives of the socialist economic organization are seen to be directed at achieving a planned social product with whatever inputs of labour, plant and materials are required. The model of capitalist objectives and its implications for organizational relations appear generally to hold in practice. However, the socialist alternative does not. The avoidance of tensions in the relation of production by means of planning oriented towards social objectives has not been achieved in socialist societies. The low productivity of labour has been a long-standing concern in countries like the USSR, and there are many complaints about poor discipline (Lampert, 1984; Pietsch, 1984). Although socialism is expected to promote a sense of collective identity within organizations, there is concern about worker motivation in socialist countries, together with evidence of considerable job dissatisfaction and illegal informal practices (Haraszti, 1977; Grancelli, 1984). This inconsistency between the expectations of the political economy model and actuality leaves an interesting question to be answered.

Capitalist ideology appeals to the notion of economic betterment through individual initiative and self-help. Although it has clearly become modified with the rise of large bureaucratic corporations, and perhaps never took deep root in more corporatist societies, capitalist ideology stands in stark contrast to its socialist counterparts. Socialist ideology emphasizes the collective. The party is seen to play the role of representing the interests of the working class as a general collective, and hence have a legitimate role in the hierarchical structures of organizations. It is regarded as appropriate that the collective view of workers in an organization, and also possibly its local community, should guide its administration and operations. Thus, within socialist organizations one would expect to find, at least in terms of formal provision, an emphasis on representing collective views, including channels for exerting influence over managerial actions to conform to collective norms. While formal channels for workers' representation are not by any means unknown in capitalist societies, and have become legally institutionalized in some, these do not have the same ideological standing in terms of providing a voice for members of the owning working class, with consequences that derive from that standing such as the right to discuss, even make, managerial appointments. Under capitalism, these and other decisions are much more likely to be claimed as managerial 'prerogatives' deriving from managers' claims to be representing ownership.

The centralization of planning and control in most socialist countries contrasts with the decentralization inherent in the use of market mechanisms. Capitalism is conducive to organizational decentralization through the establishment of internal market-allocation mechanisms on a semi-autonomous profit-centre subsidiary basis. Socialism appears to be difficult to sustain without a high degree of central direction. Kuc et al. (1980) found from a comparison of Polish, British, Japanese and Swedish factories matched for size and type of product that the centralization of decision making within the Polish organizations was considerably higher than in organizations from the three capitalist countries. They attributed this difference to the nature of direct central State involvement in enterprise planning in Poland, whereby the State establishes long-term norms for investment, pricing and resource allocation. In capitalist societies, plans or targets for such matters would normally be established within, not above, the enterprise. Also referring to Poland, Kolarska and Aldrich (1980) elaborate Hirschman's (1972) analysis of *Exit, Voice and Loyalty* by arguing that in non-market socialist societies complaint against the management of organizations has to rely on the 'indirect voice' of appealing to outside bodies (media, party) because 'exit' (working somewhere else or purchasing products from a competing enterprise) is often not possible and 'direct voice' (complaint within the enterprise) may be ineffective when decision making is centralized and therefore remote.

In capitalist societies, economic organizations are normally supervised by one- or two-tiered boards which legally represent the interests of ownership: either private shareholders or the State. In some cases, workers have a minority representation on such boards. This focal point of responsibility, which has charge of strategic policy and planning in a decentralized capitalist system, provides for a single hierarchy of executive accountable through it to the owners of capital. In contrast, socialist enterprises may be characterized as having multiple power centres and dual hierarchies. There is a managerial hierarchy responsible for plan fulfilment to a planning centre located above the enterprise. A party hierarchy parallels the managerial line within enterprises and itself reports to local and central party organizations. However, there seems to be some degree of variation in this general pattern. Laaksonen (1984), for example, reports differences in managerial influence among Chinese organizations where the general manager is also the first secretary of the party committees and where he or she is not. Lockett and Littler (1983) report variations in the extent to which factory management elections had taken place in China and, where this happened, in the degree to which nominations remained under the control of the factory director.

LABOUR MARKET AND MANAGEMENT CONTROL STRATEGIES

In recent years economists have begun to observe how labour markets tend to become stratified (Watson, 1980). Occupations may take their recruits from the 'primary sector' of what is seen as a dual market, where the work is characterized by good working conditions and pay levels, opportunities for advancement and fair treatment at work, and, especially, stability of employment. Occupations which draw on the 'secondary sector', however, are worse off in each of these respects and are particularly characterized by considerable instability and a high turnover rate (Piore, 1972). Members of this secondary workforce will tend to be people who are dispensable, possess clearly visible social differences, are little interested in training or gaining economic reward, and are ones who tend not to act collectively (Barron and Norris, 1976; Watson, 1980).

Friedman (1977a, 1977b, 1982) provides a Marxist analysis of managerial control strategies in capitalist economies and suggests how a dual labour market can be exploited by managers. He argues that in response to the changes in environment, such as varying strength of workers' resistance, new technology and market conditions (especially labour market), two types of managerial control strategies could be used in order to maintain a stable high profit. These strategies are 'responsible autonomy' and 'direct control'. Responsible autonomy involves allowing workers more discretion in doing their job, more status, light supervision, and encouraging them to identify the top managers' objectives as theirs and work responsibly. Direct control involves close supervision, little or no discretion and responsibility in workers' jobs, and centralization of decision making in the hands of a few top managers.

The chosen control strategy is dependent upon whether top managers perceive individual employees of groups or workers as 'central' or 'peripheral'. In the business world, employees are central when they are considered to be essential to the securing of high long-run profits, especially when business conditions are depressed. This centrality may derive from their skill, knowledge and contributions that they make to the managerial authority. They may also make themselves essential to the top managers through the exercise of their collective resistance. Peripheral workers are those who perform unskilled jobs with low responsibility and low status. They come from the disadvantaged sections of society and during recessions are readily laid off.

By dividing the workers into the two categories, and employing separate control strategies for each category, that is, responsible autonomy for central workers and direct control for peripheral ones, top managers can choose between the two strategies, depending on the market conditions and technological requirements, without facing resistance or difficulties.

POLITICAL ECONOMY THEORY – AN OVERALL VIEW

The main objection to the writers following this perspective is their de-emphasis of national and cultural differences and their implications for work organizations in spite of the apparent similarities in political and economic supra-structures of the societies within which they operate. Dore, Harbison and Myers and many others who draw one's attention to the importance of economic and political institutions, such as capitalism, industrialization, and labour market, are correct in emphasizing the crucial role these institutions play in shaping organization structure and policies, but their assumptions may be qualified on at least two grounds.

First, these institutions, contrary to what is implied in the political economists' arguments, are not something *beside* culture but an integral *part* of it. Take industrialization, for example. Weber (1930) argued that the 'Protestant ethic' was the underlying drive for capitalism and, indeed, for the Industrial Revolution, in mid-eighteenth century England. If Weber's thesis is correct, the Industrial Revolution could not have started in any better place than England.

According to Weber, Protestantism encourages individualism, and individual success, including economic success, in life is considered as part of a person's religious duties towards his or her Lord. It is true that Protestantism originated in Germany, but it was the English of the Industrial Revolution era who, as an individualistic people (Macfarlane, 1978), had the 'necessary' predisposition to accommodate the new religion (see also Chapter 7 for further details). So, probably, it was not by some accident of history that the English were the first nation to industrialize. One could argue in the same vein for the cultural and historical origins of labour movements and the recognition of trade unions, democracy, socialism and so on. These institutions are in most part created by the cultural values and beliefs of the peoples concerned, and in turn, reinforce and perpetuate these values and beliefs.

However, one could also note the non-cultural factors which may contribute to the formation and nature of these social phenomena.

Political economy theory 33

For instance, availability of cheap raw materials imported from the British Empire's colonies in the eighteenth century may have as much facilitated the Industrial Revolution in England as the cultural characteristics of the English.

Secondly, these social institutions, although similar in name, have a strong local cultural 'flavour', even when they are not locally originated. For instance, an examination of trade union movements in Britain, France and the United States, whose economic systems are similar (capitalist), shows that there are fundamental differences in ideology and approach between these three countries that are explainable more by their respective cultural characteristics than by their economic systems (see Jamieson, 1980, for a comparison of American and British trade union movements, and Gallie, 1978, for a comparison between British and French trade unions).

The cultural and other local differences in the societies with apparently similar ideological supra-structures are manifested in the different forms of socialism developed in China, Russia, Albania, Yugoslavia and Cuba, and the different types of capitalism existing in Britain, India and the USA. It would therefore be incorrect to assume that work organizations operating under these very different systems with similar 'labels' would employ similar management practices or respond to their environment in similar ways.

4
Cultural Theory

After a lull of nearly a decade, the late 1970s and the 1980s have seen a revival of interest by researchers in the cross-cultural study of organization. Researchers, in their attempt to examine the implications of culture for management practices and organizational structure, have generally followed two strands within the field. On the one hand there are 'ideationalists' who have directed their attention to the attitudes and values expressed by organizational members. On the other hand, 'institutionalists' in the limited amount of research they have conducted so far have concentrated upon structural aspects within organizations, such as the division of labour, career, status and reward structures. While in principle both approaches retain the holistic view of cultures inherited from anthropology, in practice they have selected a limited range of ideational 'dimensions' or particular institutional sectors for purposes of cross-national comparison (Child and Tayeb, 1983). The following sections discuss in some detail salient studies carried out within the ideational and institutional strands of the cultural perspective.

The success of Japanese managers in the past few decades has encouraged many researchers to study Japanese organizations in either single-culture frameworks or in comparative paradigms, in an attempt to establish whether or not Japan's distinctive culture accounts for the success of Japanese companies.

De Bettignies (1973) reported that cultural characteristics of Japanese people, rooted in their history and family structure, are manifested in their organizational behaviour. He argued that these deeply-rooted values influence organizational relationships in the forms of (a) a strong sense of group or community; (b) a strong sense of obligation and gratitude; (c) a strong sense of 'we' versus 'they'; (d) an underlying emotionality and excitability which is controlled by a somewhat compulsive attention to details, plans and rules; (e) a willingness to work hard and to persevere towards long-range goals; (f) a total devotion to the boss; (g) an emphasis on self-effacement and a tendency to attribute responsibilities to others rather than taking responsibility for one's own actions; and (h) a strong belief that competence comes automatically with seniority.

Ouchi (1981) compared American and Japanese organizations and found that they strongly contrasted with respect to certain characteristics that, in his view, are crucial for the effectiveness of organizations. The Japanese organizations are generally characterized by lifetime employment, slow evaluation and promotion, nonspecialized career paths, implicit control mechanisms, collective decision making, collective responsibility, and a holistic concern for people; the American organizations are generally characterized by the opposite attributes.

In his extensive review of studies of Japanese organizations, Smith (1984) concluded that the organization of work in Japan reflects the social structure of that society. A person's place of work is a major source of identity. Work organizations are structured in terms of very precise status hierarchies, but a person's position in the hierarchy is not so much a matter of the possession of certain attributes, but a matter of their membership of a particular team or category. Promotion at junior levels is largely a matter of advancement by age, but at senior levels proven ability becomes increasingly important. Subordinate members of an organization are expected to be highly committed to their work, to monitor and put right the quality of what they do, to accept willingly reassignment to other tasks, to co-operate with others in solving problems, to suggest improvements in working methods, to volunteer for overtime working, and to participate in a certain amount of after-hours socializing with work colleagues. Their motivation to fulfil these expectations is encouraged by the fact that substantial bonuses depend upon the firm's success, and that their own prestige in society is substantially linked to that of their employer. Many employees enjoy secure job tenure which also strengthens the link between their own success and that of their firm. Organizational superiors are expected to show all the above qualities and, in addition, to provide a distinctive pattern of leadership. This includes a sensitive, often indirect, concern for workforce, openness to suggestions from below, detailed technical expertise, overt criticism of task failure, a sense of personal accountability for the failure of subordinates, and the seeking out of a consensus view of events.

The heavily culturalist interpretation of Japanese management practices has, however, been disputed (Child and Tayeb, 1983). For instance, Japan's so called 'lifetime employment' system was first identified for Western readers by Abegglen (1958) who regarded it as a near-absolute moral commitment that was culturally inspired by the ideals of earlier feudal eras. Subsequent investigation, while not necessarily denying the element of cultural continuity, tends towards the conclusion that lifetime employment was instituted by large oligopolistic firms between approximately 1910 and 1930 in the light of political economy factors. In a period of growing labour militancy and high labour turnover, oligopolistic firms could attempt to secure labour commitment through offering job security and regular progression up a pay hierarchy. These firms were in a position to protect themselves from the risk of shouldering this overhead in times of poor trade by exporting any adjustment of employment levels to large numbers of small highly dependent external sub-contractors (Littler, 1982, 1983). The important point, as Child and Tayeb state, is that this dual labour market policy is comparable to that pursued by oligopolistic firms in many other countries including the United States (Loveridge and Mok, 1979; Isamu, 1981). It has also been argued that the desire of workers to remain with a single employer offering favourable conditions is not a peculiarly Japanese cultural characteristic (Marsh and Mannari, 1976).

Studies conducted by Pascale (1978) and Pascale and Maguire (1980) found few differences between successful Japanese and American organizations. The authors compared fourteen American organizations with ten Japanese ones, matching them as closely as possible. The study found that worker absenteeism was lower in Japan; Japanese managers reported more upward communication and better implementation of decisions; Japanese managers used less written communication, possibly because of the relative difficulty of typewriting in Japanese. The authors, however, concluded that Japanese organizations cannot be thought of as differing systematically from Western ones. Pascale and Athos (1982) further argued that there is a convergence in the practice of successful Western and Japanese organizations, though unsuccessful ones might well vary in different ways.

Organizations in other cultures have also come under the scrutiny of researchers, albeit to a lesser extent compared to the Japanese ones. Some of these studies have only identified distinctive characteristics of organizations, while others have tried to relate these to the cultural traits of the peoples involved. Crozier (1964, 1973), in his seminal study of French bureaucracy, attributed certain dysfunctions of the French organizations to certain cultural characteristics of French people which, he argued, were created and reinforced by various French social institutions, especially the educational system.

Four basic elements appear to be essential to the stability of the vicious circle that characterizes French organizations. These are (a) the extent of the development of impersonal rules; (b) the unusual amount of centralization; (c) the isolation of different strata; and (d) the development of parallel power relationships. These characteristics, Crozier argues, are rather well established French cultural traits. Another characteristic which he argues is peculiarly French and influences interpersonal relationships in French organizations is 'fear of face-to-face relationships'. Together with Thoenig (Crozier and

Thoenig, 1976), Crozier found that in the French system of local government and bureaucratic actions a compromise cannot be negotiated directly by the parties immediately involved. The compromise is brought about through the intervention of an external 'actor' who does not belong to any of the groups to which the parties belong.

Kakar (1971a and 1971b) reported that the paternal type of superior–subordinate relationships, especially in the form of assertive superior behaviour, dominates the authority relations in Indian organizations. He argued that this pattern is related to socio-cultural factors in Indian traditions as well as the hierarchical development of modern work organizations in India.

Chung (1978) and Nam (1971) observed South Korean managers to exhibit the Confucian virtues of familism, filial piety, and loyalty and obedience to authorities, including their leaders. England and Lee (1971) and Harbron (1979) found that South Korean managers were disinclined to adopt systems of shared management and power equalization within organizations.

Sorge and Warner (1980, 1981) found marked differences between the West German and British factories that they studied with respect to shape of organizations, functional differentiation and integration mechanisms, basic features of industrial systems, and the process of education and training. They attributed these differences to what they called 'distinct national technical culture'. Brossard and Maurice (1976) proposed a 'societal effect approach' for studying organizations. This is an extension of organizational research into the interaction of people at work, work characteristic of jobs, system of recruitment, education and training, remuneration and industrial relations. All these are considered as phenomena constituted in a society. The approach explores different courses of action towards similar goals (such as running a factory within a certain task environment), conditions under which different solutions to similar challenges are chosen by the actors, and how these solutions and actions are influenced by the societal fabric in which the actors operate.

Working within a 'societal effect' framework, Maurice, Sorge and Warner (1980), compared closely matched factories in France, West Germany and Great Britain, and remarked that organizational processes of differentiation and integration consistently interact with the processes of education, training, recruiting and promoting manpower, so that both develop within an institutional logic that is peculiar to a society, and bring about nationally different shapes of organizations.

Gallie (1978) studied work attitudes of workers in four oil refineries belonging to a multinational corporation, two situated in Britain and two in France. The refineries were matched for technology and size, and all had a low level of turnover. He found substantial contrasts in the attitudes of employees and their relations with management. In Gallie's view, the key to understanding the differences between British and French workers' attitudes and degree of integration into a company lies in the factors that are nationally specific: (a) the prevailing style and ideology of management in France is paternalistic and insistent on the preservation of managerial prerogatives; (b) the distribution of power within social institutions which is less diffused in France and which thus encourages a hostile and alienated attitude among employees; and (c) the ideology and mode of the trade union movement in each country. The major unions in Britain are closely linked to the organs of parliamentary government and do not see industrial action as a necessary medium for political change, while in France unions to a great extent do.

Jamieson (1980) studied the structural characteristics and attitudes of managers of five British companies closely matched with six American subsidiaries operating in Britain. He found significant differences between the structures of the two groups of companies and between the attitudes held by their managers. American companies reflected the more open culture of American society, tended to give more importance to the human factor, took more care in selection and appraisal of managers and training of personnel officers, made greater use of techniques of managerial control, and were more informal, more employee centred and less status conscious compared to their British counterparts. For the American companies the crucial area was marketing, and for the British ones production. Jamieson concluded that, given the findings of the study, it was not clear whether culture or economic conditions were more important in determining the structural characteristics and managerial attitudes of the two samples. He suggested that although culture is a crucial factor, the role of economic conditions is equally great.

One of the most recent studies which addressed the question of influence of culture on organizational structure was conducted by Hofstede (1980). In his investigations into the work-related attitudes and values of managers working in subsidiaries of a multinational company in thirty-nine countries, Hofstede identified four cultural dimensions along which countries can be shown to differ. These dimensions are 'power distance', 'uncertainty avoidance', 'individualism/collectivism' and 'masculinity/femininity'. He then argued that these cultural dimensions determine the way in which organizations are structured and managed.

'Power distance' is conceptually related to 'concentration of authority' (centralization). It indicates the extent to which a society accepts that power in institutions and organizations is distributed unequally. This is reflected just as much in the values of the less powerful members of the society as in the values of the more powerful ones. Some national and regional cultures are characterized by large inequality, concentration of power in the hands of small and permanent elites, centralized organizations with tall hierarchical pyramids, and restricted upward communication. Some national and regional cultures are characterized by smaller inequality, more social mobility, less concentration of power in the hands of a small elite, decentralized organizations with flatter hierarchies, and relatively free upward communication.

'Uncertainty avoidance' is related to 'structuring of activities' (formalization, specialization, standardization), and indicates the lack of tolerance in a society for uncertainty and ambiguity. This expresses itself in higher levels of anxiety and energy releases, greater need for formal rules and absolute truth and less tolerance for people or groups with deviant ideas or behaviours. Some cultures represent higher levels of activity and personal energy. The more active cultures tend to apply more specialization, formalization, and standardization in their organizations. They put a higher value on uniformity and are less tolerant of, and interested in, deviant ideas. They tend to avoid risky decisions. The less active cultures attach less importance to formal rules and specialization, are not interested in uniformity and are able to tolerate a large variety of different ideas. They more easily take risks in personal decisions.

Individualism refers to a loosely-knit social framework in society in which people are supposed to take care only of themselves and their immediate families; collectivism is one in which they can expect their relatives, clan, or work organization to look after them. More collectivist societies call for greater emotional dependence of members on their organizations. In a society in equilibrium the organizations in turn assume a broad responsibility for their members.

The predominant pattern of socialization in almost all societies is for men to be more assertive and for women to be more nurturing. Various data on the importance of work goals show near consistency on men scoring advancement and earnings as more important; women score quality of life and people higher. With respect to work goals, some societies are nearer the masculinity end of the masculinity/femininity dimension, others nearer the femininity end.

Hofstede, although he made a major contribution to the study of organizations within a culturalist approach, did not empirically investigate the relationships between the four dimensions of work-related values and attitudes and the structures of the organizations whose managers participated in the study. The relationships are conceptual and speculative. He arrived at his conclusions about the overwhelming influence of cultural factors on organizational structure on the basis of these speculations rather than 'hard' evidence. Further research is needed to explore the extent of the accuracy of his speculations and conclusions.

CULTURAL THEORY – AN OVERALL VIEW

The major strength of the cultural perspective as a whole is its recognition of (a) the important role that culture plays in shaping work-related values, attitudes and behaviours of individual members of various societies; (b) the fact that cultural values and attitudes are different in degree from one society to another, and (c) the fact that different cultural groups behave differently under similar circumstances because of the differences in their underlying values and attitudes.

This perspective, however, also has its drawbacks. First, many of the earlier studies conducted within this framework suffer from methodological inadequacies. A vast majority of the authors of cross-cultural studies claim to have investigated the influence of culture on organizations, but they have not made any effort to study the cultural settings of the organizations concerned. Instead when they failed to attribute the observed differences between organizations in two or more countries to non-cultural variables, they offered culture as an explanation for these differences. As Child (1981: 306) points out, these researchers treated culture as 'a residual factor which is presumed to account for national variations that have neither been postulated before the research nor explained after its completion'.

Secondly, no effort has been made to disentangle organizations' own culture from the culture of the society within which they operate. This, as Evan (1975) points out, limits the extent to which one can claim that the variations found in comparative studies are due to societal culture, because it could be due to organizational subculture. A major exception to be noted here is Hofstede's study which was conducted in the subsidiaries of a multinational corporation in thirty-nine countries, and in which organizational sub-culture was to some extent held constant.

Thirdly, there is a marked lack of a systematic study of the cultural values and attitudes of the people concerned through both an investigation into the historical development of those values and attitudes, and an independent survey of the cultural traits of a sample of ordinary people outside the organizations which are to be studied, and those of a sample of the employees of the organizations, in order to examine the coherence between the cultural values and the organizationally-relevant attitudes and values of the people involved. Terry's (1979) study of English culture and values held by a sample of English managers has to some extent paid attention to this point. However, he used literature and the findings of the empirical surveys conducted by other researchers (notably Gorer, 1955) on English culture as his source material to establish the cultural traits present in the English.

Fourthly, there is a relative lack of reported studies that have attempted to examine the relationship between specific culturally-influenced work-related values and attitudes and specific structural variables (except Hofstede, 1980 to some extent).

Fifthly, many studies engaged in cross-cultural research have treated heterogeneous cultures as unified and homogeneous simply because they coexist within politically determined national boundaries. Take Britain for example. It consists of four major distinct cultural peoples, namely, the English, the Irish, the Scottish and the Welsh. Also, there are many more immigrant minorities who, along with the major groups, staff, run and own the so-called British organizations. How is one to know, for instance, that the 'British' organization which is compared with, say, an Indian company, is not in fact staffed largely by immigrants from the sub-continent? Considerations such as these set limits to the validity of any generalization based on a comparison between British culture (or any other heterogeneous culture for that matter) and that of other countries.

Sixthly, culturalists tend to over-emphasize the role of culture in organization to the neglect of the importance of the commercial, non-cultural environment which surrounds the organization and imposes its own demands and 'imperatives' on the organization. As Caves (1980) points out, it is important for the organization to respond to its environment if it is to be viable. It is a gross mistake, committed by many culturalist researchers, to assume that an organization is shaped only by the cultural values of its members, and that the economic and task environment does not play a significant role in the process.

5
Organization and Culture: A Hypothetical Model

The concepts which are most central to the present study are culture and organizational structure. These concepts have aroused controversy and confusion among various scholars as to their precise meaning. For instance, Kroeber and Kluckhohn (1952) cited 164 different definitions of culture. Mintzberg (1979: 13) recalls that after reading over 200 books and articles for the first draft of *The Structuring of Organizations* '... I was not really sure what structure was. I found myself groping for a frame of reference.'

In the light of this confusion, the present author decided to develop her own definitions of culture and organizational structure, with three criteria in mind: (a) the definitions should give the reader an insight to my understanding of these concepts: (b) they should ensure that the reader and author will have the same meanings in mind whenever they encounter these concepts in the book: and (c) they can be related to the hypotheses of the study in a straightforward manner.

CULTURE AND ITS SCOPE

Culture is defined as a set of historically evolved learned values and attitudes and meanings shared by the members of a given community that influences their material and non-material way of life. Members of the community learn these shared characteristics through different stages of the socialization processes of their lives in institutions, such as family, religion, formal education and society as a whole. Not all the individual members of the community need necessarily be assumed to follow all the directives of their cultures in every aspect of their lives. There are variations within a given culture. One can distinguish between individual variations and the dominant general pattern. What is important to note is that the dominant social pattern of a given culture is a recognizable whole which may differ in significant ways from another recognizable whole in another place or time.

The differences that exist between various cultures are of degree rather than of kind, and cultural values and attitudes can be considered in terms of dimensions placed on continua ranging from low to high. For instance, sexual discrimination against women is a socio-cultural dimension common to almost all societies. However, the extent of this discrimination varies from one society to another.

ORGANIZATIONAL STRUCTURE

The decision making process is viewed as a base on and around which the organization is 'built'. An organization comes into being when a person or a group of persons decides to achieve certain goals in collaboration with one or more persons. Decisions are then made on the ways and means by which these goals are to be achieved. Subsequent activities of the organization are all based on the decisions which are made by the people concerned. The 'death' of the organization is again the outcome of a decision.

Organizational structure is regarded as a framework for decision making and decision implementation. An understanding of structure, therefore, requires reference not only to such dimensions as centralization, specialization and formalization (Pugh et al., 1968), but also to the relationships, processes and actions which lie behind these dimensions. These relationships and processes are power and authority relationships, coping with uncertainty and risk-taking, interpersonal trust, loyalty and commitment, motivation, control and discipline, co-ordination and integration, communication, consultation and participation.

An example can clarify this definition of organizational structure. A high degree of centralization taken on its own means nothing other than that many decisions are taken by a few managers at the top of the organizational hierarchy. It does not reflect the amount of consultation and information exchange that takes place before the decisions are made. The degree to which consultation and information exchange occurs depends on the managers' philosophy, on their trust in the employees, and on the latter's ability and willingness to participate in the decision-making process. Centralization does not reflect how much power the actors involved actually have. Decisions apparently taken by senior managers may well have been influenced by those employees who do not hold any formal position of power, but, because of, say, their expertise, can actually exert a great deal of pressure and control on the decision makers.

In the present study, the formal dimensions of structure are referred to as the etic aspects, and their underlying processes and relationships as the emic aspects of organizations. It is the emic aspects that, it is argued, reflect and are influenced by the culture of the society within which an organization operates.

The following sections hypothesize the likely interaction between etic and emic aspects of organizational structure and the role of culture in this interaction. The model presented in the sections is based on cultural theory and expands on Hofstede's (1980) thesis with respect to the implications of power distance, uncertainty avoidance and individualism for organizational structure, and the author's (Tayeb, 1979, 1984) arguments about the influence of employees' commitment and interpersonal trust on organizational structure and management control systems. The model will then be put to the test. It is assumed that if it holds true for the participating organizations, the cultural theory offers a valid and adequate explanation for these organizations' characteristics.

Power and authority relationships in organizations

In a decision-making situation involving at least two actors, various power and authority scenarios can be envisaged. A decision may be taken by one person and the order for its implementation carried by the other (unequal power relationship). In a second scenario, the two actors may take the decision together and contribute to its implementation (equal power relationship). In a third scenario a combination of these two forms may be in operation. One of the factors which may influence the adoption by or existence in the organizations of any of these power patterns is the generally-followed pattern of senior–junior power relationships in the society of which the two 'actors' are members. Child–parent, human–God, pupil–teacher and subject–king relationships are some examples of the power relationship patterns in which an individual is placed in his or her various capacities by the society's norms and customs. These norms and customs are built and reinforced in socio-cultural institutions and are peculiar to a given society.

Following a culturalist perspective, it is argued that if in a society in general there is a wide power and authority 'gap' between seniors and juniors, the same pattern is reflected in an unequal power relationship between superiors and subordinates in work organizations in that society, in the form of high centralization and low consultation. The opposite pattern would be the case in the societies with more equal and diffused power relationships.

Tolerance for ambiguity

Most managerial decisions involve some degree of risk taking. The more uncertain are the conditions under which the decisions are taken, the greater will be the risk involved and the greater will be the uncertainty about the correctness of the decisions and the consequences of their outcome. Participation in a decision-making situation depends to some degree on an individual's ability to cope with this uncertainty. This ability in turn may depend, among other things, on the individual's tolerance for ambiguity (Adorno et al., 1950; Berlyne, 1968). The degree of tolerance for ambiguity influences the behaviour of the individual in the face of uncertainty, and also the mechanism that he or she employs to cope with it. Fromm (1942), for instance, explained Fascism and Nazism by a need to 'escape from freedom', a response to anxiety which freedom created in societies with low tolerance for such anxiety.

An individual may have a low tolerance for ambiguity and choose to 'buffer' himself against it. A person may have a high tolerance for ambiguity and choose to face up to it and fight it. The roots of that passive defensive action and this aggressive way of coping with uncertainty lie to a great extent in the experience of the individual through different stages of his life. This experience is expected to be influenced by the collectively shared characteristics of the people among whom the individual is brought up.

Organizations as decision-making structures provide numerous cases where the individuals involved have to handle uncertainty. It can be argued that in societies with low tolerance for uncertainty, organizational members will display not only this cultural tendency but also the mechanism by which they can buffer themselves against the uncertainty. This mechanism manifests itself in greater use of rules and regulations and detailed definitions of areas of discretion and responsibility. In societies with greater tolerance for uncertainty one would expect to see a lower degree of formalization and job definition in work organizations.

Commitment

The concept of organizational commitment refers to a person's affective reactions to characteristics of his employing organization. It is concerned with feelings of attachment to the goals and values of the organization, one's role in relation to this, and attachment to the organization for its own sake rather than for its strictly instrumental value (Cook and Wall, 1980).

Commitment has a significant implication for management control system. If employees' commitment to an organization is low, managers may have to enhance it by adopting appropriate motivational measures and increasing control and supervision over employees both directly and indirectly.

The willingness to commit oneself to the organization and to accept responsibility and participate in decision making may be broken down into two components: group-orientation and motivation.

Group-orientation

It is important, though not sufficient, that the individual who is expected to contribute to the achievement of a collective purpose should have a rather high sense of co-operation. The strength of this sense of co-operation depends, it is assumed, on whether the individual is self-oriented (individualist) or group-oriented (collectivist).

If a self-oriented person belonged to a group, her attachment to the group's interests would be loose, her group would not be the centre of her loyalty, and she might be biased in her relationships with the group. This is especially true if she did not perceive any convergence between her personal interests and those of the group. In this case she would not contribute to the achievement of the group's interests and goals.

A group-oriented person has a strong feeling of belonging to the group of which she is a member. She is therefore more likely to perceive a positive relation between her personal goals and those of the group and is expected to participate actively in the achievement of the collective goals of the group. A group-oriented person is attached to her group as the centre of her life.

In this connection Hofstede (1980) and Triandis (1981) have drawn attention to the concepts of 'ingroup' and 'outgroup'. The scope of ingroup and domain of outgroup denote the extent to which an individual is prepared to have 'close' or 'distant' relationships with others, and the extent to which others will be the object of her loyalty. In some cultures ingroup consists of only family members (for example, Iran, especially in large cities); in some it encompasses close relations and friends too (for example, India); and in some societies it includes also one's work organization (for example, Japan).

Motivation

Employees participate in the decision-making process if, given their skill and knowledge, they are motivated. One way of motivating employees is to satisfy or promise to satisfy their expectations of the job. These expectations and what the employees consider as important are assumed to be consistent with their cultural backgrounds. For example, in a predominantly individualistic society employees are expected to consider independence, autonomy and privacy at work as more important than would employees from a predominantly collectivistic society. The latter may attach more importance to a sense of belonging.

Having discussed the two components of commitment, it is assumed that, following a cultural perspective, in societies with weaker commitment to collective activities and lower preference for autonomy and discretion, organizational members are less likely to involve themselves in decision making and to participate in the achievement of their organization's goals. Power in organizations is consequently less diffused, and control and discipline are more direct, external and coercive. This would then probably create a self-reinforcing system of low commitment and tight control.

Trust

Trust refers to the extent to which one is willing to ascribe good intentions to and confidence in the words and actions of other people (Cook and Wall, 1980). Trust, too, has significant implications for management control systems. The lower the management's trust in the employees' abilities and intentions, the more likely it is that the former increases its direct control over the latter and the less likely will it delegate decision making power to them.

It is hypothesized that in societies with low interpersonal trust, the structure of organizations is expected to be centralized. In cultures with a higher degree of interpersonal trust, organizations would tend to have relatively decentralized structures.

There are other factors besides commitment and trust which may influence management control systems. The power of those who are affected by these systems is one such factor. There may be countervailing collective actions by the employees and their unions which attempt to negotiate over control systems. Also, organizational members may have the power to mould the control rules and systems and establish informal practices. These and similar actions are manifestations of the challenge to power and authority and are argued to be influenced by the cultural backgrounds of the organizational members.

Communication

Communication in an organization is maintained either through vertical or lateral channels or a combination of both. The present study intends to investigate the extent to which communication systems are culture-bound. In some cultures the dominant pattern may be vertical; in others lateral as well as vertical. It is hypothesized that communication pattern as a cultural trait is also present in work organizations.

Table 5.1 summarizes the hypotheses advanced in this chapter about the processes through which culture may influence organizational structures and control systems.

Table 5.1 *Hypothetical process of influence of culture on organizational structure and systems*

Predominant cultural value	Characteristics of organization structure
Small power distance	Low centralization High consultation
Large power distance	High centralization Low consultation
High tolerance for ambiguity	Low centralization Low structuring (low formalization, low standardization, non-specific definition of areas of discretion and responsibility, low specialization)
Low tolerance for ambiguity	High centralization High structuring (high formalization, high standardization, specific definition of areas of discretion and responsibility, high specialization)
High commitment	Low centralization Relaxed, internalized control
Low commitment	High centralization Severe, external control
High trust	Low centralization Relaxed, internalized control
Low trust	High centralization Severe, external control

PART III
CULTURAL AND ORGANIZATIONAL ASSESSMENT

6
Research Design and Methodology

Many of the studies conducted in the past within a culturalist framework suffer from methodological inadequacies which make their conclusions less than reliable. The researchers have simply investigated a few aspects of a group of loosely matched organizations across two or more cultures. Without surveying (a) the cultural characteristics of the peoples concerned independently, and (b) the work attitudes of the members of the organizations, they have attributed, post hoc, the differences in the structural properties of the organizations under study to the differences of the cultures involved. Furthermore, these studies have not examined the implications of given aspects of culture for specific aspects of organizational structure.

In the present study, attempts were made to overcome these methodological drawbacks. The study employed a nomothetic cross-national design, utilizing the principle of matching, whereby a sample of organizations were matched on contingency and political economy factors, and the influence of cultural factors on their organizations' structural features was studied. This design strategy recognizes and incorporates the importance of various factors suggested by three theoretical perspectives (see Chapters 2 to 4) as having bearings on organizations. The following steps were taken to implement this design:

1 Identify certain cultural values and attitudes which could be theoretically related to certain aspects of organizational structure and articulate the model of associations between these two sets of variables (Chapter 5).
2 Assess the culture of the peoples involved through (a) a study of the available literature, supplemented by personal observations; and (b) the administration of an independent survey of the values and attitudes of a sample of the populations of the countries concerned (Chapter 7).

3 Administer a work-related attitudes survey among members of a group of organizations (Chapters 8 and 9). The respondents in step 2 would not be the same as those in step 3. This strategy would allow an examination of the coherence (or otherwise) between the culture of the people involved as members of a society and the work-related attitudes held by them as members of organizations.

4 Select a sample of organizations in one country and match them in pairs with another sample from at least one other country (England and India). The matching would be on major contextual variables. These organizations would be the ones whose members' work attitudes would be studied in the earlier stage of the research. These organizations would be studied in detail in order to examine the influence of certain work-related attitudes of their members for specific aspects of their structures.

Table 6.1 shows the factors and variables which were studied. Employees work-related attitudes and organizations' structures and control systems were the dependent variables; cultural factors, both ideational and institutional, were independent variables; and the variables which were controlled were the contingency and contextual factors, and, to some extent, the political economic factors.

The final part of the design of the study was to devise a methodology to collect the required data. This methodology is discussed in the following sections. It should be pointed out at this stage that my Iranian cultural background placed me in a position from which I was able to observe those aspects of Indian and English societies which might be taken for granted by the native members of each population. Furthermore, I tried to enhance my sensitivity and understanding of the two cultures through discussions with people from the two countries about my interpretations of various aspects of their societies and cultures, as well as through reading books and articles by native writers about their own countries.

RESEARCH METHODOLOGY

The fieldwork was carried out in three stages in each country: cultural surveys, work-related attitudes surveys, and organizational structures surveys. The remainder of this chapter is accordingly divided into three parts which describe the methodology employed at each stage of the fieldwork.

Table 6.1 *Factors selected to be examined in the study*

Organizational variables	Contingency and contextual factors	Political–economic factors	Cultural factors
Centralization	Industry	Economic system	Primary and secondary social institutions: family, religion, education, political regime, class structure, mass media, labour movement
Perceived autonomy	Product	Existence of trade unions	
Specialization	Technology	Industrialization	Cultural attitudes and values
Formalization	Market share		Work-related attitudes and values: attitude to power and authority
Chief executive's span of control	Size		tolerance for ambiguity
	Age		commitment
Height	Ownership		trust
			individualism
Communication pattern	Control		expectations from job
			attitude to others
Control systems	Status		attitude to control systems
			information sharing
Reward and punishment policies			attitude to participation

Cultural and organizational assessment

CULTURAL SURVEYS

Observations

My stay in England since 1976 gave me ample opportunity, both as a participant and non-participant observer, to learn about the English and their way of life. My visit to India was for a much shorter period; I lived there for just over four months from mid-February to late June 1983.

In both countries, I watched and listened to television and radio programmes, and read systematically daily and weekly national papers and journals catering for the interests of different social groups and tastes. As a participant observer, I became actively involved in formal and informal political and social activities, such as attending demonstrations, rallies and meetings, religious gatherings and debates. I travelled extensively and went on organized tours and small group holidays with people from different social backgrounds, and spent time with families in their homes as an invited or paying guest.

Questionnaire

I commenced by reading literature on English and Indian cultures and social institutions to find out about the salient characteristics of their respective peoples. I supplemented my literature search with unstructured and informal interviews with people from different walks of life in order to construct a sound basis for a cultural survey questionnaire. The questionnaire consisted of two parts. The first part contained questions devised to check the country of origin and to ascertain the occupational background of the respondents. The main body of the questionnaire consisted of thirty-five pairs of opposing characteristics. The items had been selected on the basis of their salience in the two cultures. They were also related to the issues and relationships involved in work organizations and among their members. The areas covered in the questionnaire were acceptance of responsibility, honesty and trust, attitudes towards senior people, independence, group-orientation, self-confidence and resourcefulness, ability to cope with uncertainty, tolerance, friendliness, fair play, fatalism, social stratification and attitudes towards the law.

The respondents in each country were asked to rate people in their own occupation, rather than themselves, on a seven-point scale provided for each pair. The question was a projective one because people are likely to be more honest and frank when they describe others in terms of the characteristics included in the present study than they are when they describe themselves.

Each pair of the characteristics was placed in the questionnaire in such a way as to minimize unconscious response sets. The form and language of the questionnaire were determined after informal interviews with some twenty men and women. Suggestions and comments on earlier drafts were also received from ten other people, all from different educational and social backgrounds.

The same questionnaire was used in both the English and Indian survey. This facilitated the comparison between the two samples. However, it must be pointed out that because different cultures may attach different meanings to given terms and concepts, the use of the same questionnaire may render particular questions non-comparable in terms of interpretations by respondents. This is a difficulty which is encountered in attempting cross-cultural comparisons. However, the author tried to overcome this problem by, as mentioned above, complementing the survey with literature research, observations, and discussions with local people.

The questionnaire was administered in English and Hindi versions. The Hindi version was translated from the English draft by a college professor, and then translated back into English by a different person. After necessary modification, it was typed and printed. In the case of illiterate respondents my Indian friends who could speak the respondents' language helped with the interpretations.

The questionnaire was piloted in both England and India among twenty people in each country from various walks of life.

Sampling procedures

English sample
England is said to be a 'class-ridden' society, and, furthermore, there are differences in the strength of the values and attitudes attributed to the members of different classes (Gorer, 1955; Terry, 1979). The sample had therefore to be broadly representative of class membership. Many factors, such as occupation, educational background, parental background, income and housing conditions, are said to indicate the social class to which a person 'belongs'. Of these factors, occupation was chosen as the basis of class differentiation in the present study, because it is largely influenced by educational and family background, and in turn determines the level of income.

The majority of the population of the country could be 'placed' in two very broad classes, namely, middle and working classes. For the purpose of drawing up a sample, non-manual workers were taken to represent middle-class people and the manual workers to represent working-class people. According to the 1971 census, which was the most recent available when this study commenced, 47 percent of the

54 *Cultural and organizational assessment*

economically active population were engaged in non-manual work and 53 percent in manual occupations (Reid, 1977). The proportion of the middle- and working-class people in the sample was exactly as that of the country as a whole. Moreover, the composition of the manual workers' section of the sample was also matched in terms of skill category with that of the national distribution – 22 percent skilled, 23 percent semi-skilled, and 8 percent unskilled workers.

Indian sample
India is a vast country with a total population of around 700 million who are said to have different cultural and social characteristics, depending on their religions, castes and the regions from which they come. However, the kind of attitudes and values the survey intended to examine were general and broad and were mainly related to familial and social relationships which, according to the literature and observers' accounts (for example, Gore, 1965; Koestler, 1966; Kakar, 1971a and 1971b; Lannoy, 1971; Segal, 1971; Parekh, 1974; Hiro, 1976) were more-or-less the same across different social and regional groups and communities.

Given the vastness of the country, the time and financial constraints, the limited availability of interpreters, and the methodological considerations to be discussed shortly, it was decided to limit the sample to the following groups:

People from urban areas Organization members are drawn from the urban population and therefore the culture of this population would be the appropriate culture to be studied. If the rural population were to be represented in the sample, it would have distorted the analyses of the findings of the survey of the organization employees. Any discrepancy between the findings of the two studies could have been interpreted as a confirmation of the 'culture-free' thesis, although it might quite possibly have been a consequence of differences between the two (rural and urban) cultures. In order to avoid this confusion it was decided to exclude the rural population from the sample.

Hindus Religion plays a significant role in the upbringing of Indian children and the formation of Indian culture as a whole. Since Hinduism is the religion to which the majority of the population, around 83 percent, adhere, it was decided to confine the sample largely to Hindus.

People from Maharashtra and near-by states The choice of these areas was influenced by the fact that the second and third stages of the research, that is the surveys of employee's work-related attitudes and organizational structure, were to be carried out in Maharashtra, which is the industrial heartland of India. It would therefore be more appropriate to choose the sample from the same cultural area in which the organizations and their members were located. It must be repeated here that those who participated in the work-related attitude survey were, of course, different from those who participated in the cultural survey.

Caste Caste is another influential factor in the cultural configuration of Indian people. However, choosing a representative sample of the population on the basis of caste proved to be virtually impossible. First, there is no information, reliable or otherwise, about the proportion of the members of each of the four broad castes and the 'Untouchables' in the total population. Secondly, each caste is divided into numerous sub-castes. As Ghurye (1932) estimates, there are at least 2,000 sub-castes in each linguistic area. The complication is further magnified by the fact that there are at least 14 official languages and hundreds of dialects spoken by 700 million people (Government of India, 1982), about whose proportion in the total population or any one state no information was available. Given this situation, it was decided to drop caste as a measure of representativeness of the sample, and instead to choose occupation.

Occupation The choice of occupation was also justified on another ground. Divisions between castes are broadly, albeit not invariably, based on occupation. Although members of the same occupation do come from different castes or sub-castes, it is possible to argue that the unequal status and privileges associated with different castes provide unequal opportunities for their members. Again, although there are exceptional cases, such as the rise of an 'Untouchable' to the post of Cabinet Minister in the Janata Government, the more general rule is that it is unlikely that an out-caste butcher or cobbler would be able to send his child to the prestigious schools and colleges from which the bulk of would-be administrators, lawyers, lecturers, managers and the like graduate. It is more likely that the holders of these occupations come from higher castes such as Kshatrya or Brahmin.

By taking occupation as the criterion for social background of the Indian sample the sampling rationale for the study is placed on the same basis as that of the English study, and therefore permits culture to be the major differentiating feature of the two samples.

Applying the same sampling rationale as in England would have meant choosing an occupational distribution to match that of the population of the country, or the selected region, as a whole. However, in the absence of any reliable information about the breakdown of occupational groups, it was decided to include in the sample as many occupations as was practically possible and, further, to draw an arbitrary line between manual and non-manual workers at the 50–50 point.

Sample size

The sample in each country consisted of a hundred people from all walks of life whose occupation and social background were as near as possible in the same proportion as that of the whole of the population of their respective country. In England, 140 copies of the questionnaire had to be completed by the people who were approached up and down the country before a representative sample was achieved. In India, 130 copies were completed before the required sample was obtained.

Administration of the surveys, including the pilot studies, took eight months from August 1980 to February 1981 in England, and just over four months from mid-February to late June 1983 in India.

A limitation of these surveys was the small size of the samples. However, the objective of the exercise was not to establish English and Indian cultural traits; rather, it was to examine and verify some of these traits. As will be seen in Chapter 7, the findings of the surveys are remarkably consistent with what many writers have attributed to English and Indian people in general.

WORK-RELATED ATTITUDES SURVEYS

As will be discussed later, fourteen manufacturing companies in England and India – seven companies in each country – participated in the study. It was intended to study their structures and control strategies as well as certain work-related attitudes of a sample of their members.

The attitudes questionnaire

The questionnaire was divided into two broad sections. The first section contained eight sampling questions. The main body of the questionnaire consisted of eighty-seven items. These items, which were conceptually related to the hypotheses and arguments of the study, were designed by the author or adopted from the work of other researchers. The items were selected to be included in the questionnaire after an earlier survey carried out in Iran (Tayeb, 1979) and a pilot study conducted in England. The respondents in these earlier studies were, respectively, sixty-two members of a state-owned organization situated in Tehran, and eighty members of a university department situated in Birmingham. The final version of the questionnaire was decided after a series of statistical tests, such as correlation, factor analysis and internal reliability, was carried out on the data obtained from these two studies.

The eighty-seven items in the main body of the questionnaire covered the following issues: power and authority, ambiguity and uncertainty, commitment, interpersonal trust, individualism, expectations from a job, attitudes to management practices, perceived autonomy and communication pattern. The last two sections were included in the questionnaire to provide information about organizational structure to complement the information to be obtained in the third stage of the research. All the questions had a Likert-type answer scale and were placed in the questionnaire in such a manner as to help prevent set pattern answers.

The questionnaire was devised in English and was later translated into Hindi for administration in Indian companies. Managerial and other members of staff, who like all educated Indians, had a good command of English language, completed the English version of the questionnaire. Copies of the Hindi version were distributed among manual workers who could better comprehend this language.

An Indian professor translated the work attitudes survey into Hindi, and then a different person translated it back into English. After making necessary changes and modifications in the wording, the questionnaire was finalized.

In England, 100 copies of the questionnaire were handed or posted to the managing director of each of the seven companies which participated in the study; 376 copies of the questionnaire were completed and returned to me directly by the employees in the self-addressed stamped envelopes provided – a response rate of 53.7 percent. Distribution and return of the completed copies took nine months from October 1981 to June 1982.

In India, on the basis of the experience with the English companies, it was decided to administer sixty copies of the English version of the questionnaire in each company. One company would accept only fifty copies, giving a total of 410 English copies distributed. Three companies agreed to also distribute sixty-five copies of the Hindi version of the questionnaire (twenty, twenty, twenty-five respectively) among their employees. The questionnaires were handed to the managing directors and the completed copies, 341 in all, were collected from them a few weeks later, or posted to me in England. The response rate was 71.7 percent. Distribution, collection and return of the completed copies took five months from mid-February to mid-July 1983.

Validation of the questions

A number of the items included in the questionnaire were to be used as composite measures on the basis of which groups of employees within and between the two cultures could be compared. Statistical tests of the data from the pilot and main studies however showed that there was a poor consistency among the items of a few of these 'composite' measures, and the items could not be used collectively as scale. Table 6.2 shows that the scales for tolerance of ambiguity, commitment and trust had a sufficiently high reliability coefficient to be considered as composite measures; the constituent items of the others have to be treated individually in the analysis.

Table 6.2 *Validation of attitudes survey measures*

Measures	English data		Indian data	
	Alpha	K–R8	Alpha	K–R8
Power distance*	0.16	–	0.32	–
Perceived power	0.15	0.41	0.23	0.45
Uncertainty avoidance*	−0.26	–	−0.01	–
Tolerance of ambiguity	0.69	0.78	0.52	0.63
Individualism	0.18	0.51	0.21	0.51
Commitment	0.84	0.88	0.60	0.70
Trust	0.81	0.85	0.78	0.83
Perceived autonomy	0.33	0.60	0.39	0.64

* It was not possible to carry out a K–R8 test for the items in these measures because the answer scales for the items were not similar.

The author was perhaps one of the few researchers who used Hofstede's scales for Power Distance and Uncertainty Avoidance before the publication of his *Culture's Consequences* (Tayeb, 1979). These scales were also included in the present study to test their instrumental validity in a small scale cross-cultural research. The following sub-sections present the findings of the study with this respect.

Power distance and uncertainty avoidance measures

These measures consist of seven and ten items respectively (Chapter 8, Tables 8.2 to 8.4 and 8.8), and are conceptually related to power relationships between subordinates and their superior (power distance items) and coping with uncertainty (uncertainty avoidance items).

Factor analysis, internal reliability and correlation tests were carried out on these items for each country separately in order to examine the degree of consistency among each set of items.

Power distance items
The principal component factor analysis showed that for each sample the items collapsed into three factors. But as Tables 6.3 and 6.4 show the pattern of factors was dissimilar in the two samples and the loadings were very low in both cases.

Table 6.3 *Power distance – factor analysis (English sample)*
Varimax rotated factor matrix after rotation with kaiser normalization

Items	Factor 1 (loading)	Factor 2 (loading)	Factor 3 (loading)
1 If an employee took a complaint to a person higher than his/her own boss, do you think he/she would suffer later for doing this?	0.47	−0.0008	−0.03
2 How often is your immediate boss concerned to help you getting ahead?	0.35	−0.008	−0.14
3 How often in your experience are employees afraid to disagree with their boss?	0.62	−0.05	0.16
4 Preferred boss	−0.12	0.28	0.25
5 Perceived boss	0.004	0.06	0.60
6 Employees should participate more in decisions made by their bosses	−0.009	−0.29	−0.01
7 Employees lose respect for the boss who asks them for their advice before he makes a decision	−0.01	0.69	0.06

Note: Alpha for all 7 items = 0.16.

An Alpha internal reliability test showed a coefficient of 0.16 for the English sample and 0.32 for the Indian sample. This indicates inconsistency among the items. This inconsistency is evident in the pattern of responses to the items (see Chapter 8, Tables 8.2 to 8.4): responses given by members of the same sample to some questions would indicate a large power distance, and to others a small power distance.

The Pearson correlation test showed poor correlations between the items in both samples. The highest coefficient in the English sample was 0.28 ($p < 0.001$) between 'fear of the boss' and 'complaining employees', and in the Indian sample was 0.48 ($p < 0.001$) between 'preferred boss' and 'perceived boss'.

Uncertainty avoidance items
The factor analysis showed that the items collapsed into four factors in the English sample and five factors in the Indian sample. The

Table 6.4 *Power distance – factor analysis (Indian sample)*
Varimax rotated factor matrix after rotation with kaiser normalization

Items	Factor 1 (loading)	Factor 2 (loading)	Factor 3 (loading)
1 If an employee took a complaint to a person higher than his/her own boss, do you think he/she would suffer later for doing this?	0.0	0.10	0.32
2 How often is your immediate boss concerned to help you getting ahead?	−0.03	0.09	0.16
3 How often in your experience are employees afraid to disagree with their boss?	0.05	−0.19	0.37
4 Preferred boss	0.76	0.22	0.03
5 Perceived boss	0.60	−0.02	−0.01
6 Employees should participate more in decisions made by their bosses	−0.01	−0.03	0.30
7 Employees lose respect for the boss who asks them for their advice before he makes a decision	0.15	0.70	0.03

Note: Alpha = 0.32.

factor loadings were very low. Tables 6.5 and 6.6 show the results. The Alpha coefficient was −0.21 for the English sample and −0.01 for the Indian sample – an indication of very poor consistency among the items.

The Pearson correlation also showed the same result. The highest coefficient in the English sample was −0.37 ($p < 0.001$) between 'job satisfaction' and 'how long to stay with the company', and −0.35 ($p < 0.01$) between the same items in the Indian sample.

Hofstede has constructed power distance and uncertainty avoidance indices using three 'core' items from each set of items.

Power distance index (PDI) core items
The first item measures the extent to which the respondent is afraid to disagree with his boss. The other two items use a description of four types of boss, corresponding to Tannenbaum and Schmidt's (1958) 'tells', 'sells', 'consults', and 'joins' styles of leadership. The respondent is then asked to indicate first, to which type his own boss most closely corresponds, and second, under which type he prefers to work. A power distance index for a country is computed on the basis of its mean scores for these three questions: (a) non-managerial employees' perception that employees are afraid to disagree with their boss; (b) subordinates' perception that their boss tends to take decisions in an autocratic (tells) or persuasive (sells) manner: and (c) subordinates' preference for anything but consultative style.

Table 6.5 *Uncertainty avoidance – factor analysis (English sample)*

Varimax rotated factor matrix after rotation with kaiser normalization

Items	Factor 1 (loading)	Factor 2 (loading)	Factor 3 (loading)	Factor 4 (loading)
1 How often do you feel nervous or tense at work?	−0.27	−0.09	0.13	0.30
2 How long do you think you will continue to work for this organization?	−0.53	−0.04	−0.04	−0.02
3 If you had a choice of promotion to either a managerial or specialist position, and these were at the same salary level, which would appeal to you most?	−0.18	−0.11	0.26	−0.04
4 How do you feel about working for a boss who is from a country other than your own?	0.01	0.04	−0.10	0.52
5 Considering everything, how would you rate your overall satisfaction with this organization at the present time?	0.76	0.13	−0.17	−0.07
6 Decisions made by individuals are usually of a higher quality than decisions made by groups	0.08	0.61	−0.06	−0.05
7 Company rules should not be broken even when the employee thinks it is in the company's best interest	0.26	0.08	0.20	−0.14
8 Most organizations will be better off if conflict can be eliminated	0.08	−0.02	0.41	−0.03
9 Employees lose respect for the boss who asks them for their advice before he makes a decision	−0.09	−0.52	−0.10	−0.05
10 Competition between employees usually does more harm than good	−0.11	0.18	0.60	0.01

Note: Alpha for all 10 items = −0.26.

Hofstede excludes managers' answers to the first item in the computation because 'managers' perceptions of employees' fear to disagree are not the same as employees' perceptions: they may be distorted by low sensitivity or wishful thinking precisely in those cases where employees are very afraid' (1980: 136). This means that part of the PDI score includes managers' responses, and part of it does not. Moreover, if one wants to calculate the PDI for managers in an organization, the index is based on their responses to only two items (perceived and preferred bosses). It is questionable how responses to only two items can reflect a group of employees' attitudes to power and authority.

Table 6.6 *Uncertainty avoidance – factor analysis (Indian sample)*

Varimax rotated factor matrix after rotation with kaiser normalization

Items	Factor 1 (loading)	Factor 2 (loading)	Factor 3 (loading)	Factor 4 (loading)	Factor 5 (loading)
1 How often do you feel nervous or tense at work?	−0.04	0.05	0.01	0.13	−0.07
2 How long do you think you will continue to work for this organization?	−0.46	0.11	−0.06	0.08	−0.01
3 If you had a choice of promotion to either a managerial or specialist position, and these were at the same salary level, which would appeal to you most?	0.03	0.04	0.44	0.11	0.04
4 How do you feel about working for a boss who is from a country other than your own?	−0.006	−0.02	0.01	−0.04	0.43
5 Considering everything, how would you rate your overall satisfaction with this organization at the present time?	0.71	0.02	0.08	−0.15	−0.001
6 Decisions made by individuals are usually of a higher quality than decisions made by groups	0.25	−0.36	−0.01	0.35	−0.02
7 Company rules should not be broken even when the employee thinks it is in the company's best interest	0.002	−0.38	0.39	−0.17	−0.08
8 Most organizations will be better off if conflict can be eliminated	0.07	−0.05	0.45	−0.04	−0.009
9 Employees lose respect for the boss who asks them for their advice before he makes a decision	−0.05	0.67	−0.01	0.003	−0.09
10 Competition between employees usually does more harm than good	−0.13	−0.02	0.0006	0.28	0.01

Note: Alpha = −0.01.

Further, Hofstede does not explain why he has chosen the above three items as constituents of his formula; presumably because 'the statistical analysis shows that across the thirty-nine HERMES (the pseudonym for the multinational company in which the study was conducted) countries, the percentage of employees preferring certain types of manager is correlated with the perceptions both of employees being afraid and of managers being autocratic or persuasive/paternalistic' (p. 102). However, as will be discussed later, the correlations between these items for the present data were very poor.

Uncertainty avoidance index (UAI) core items
These items refer to three components of national level of uncertainty avoidance: rule orientation, employment stability, and stress. On the country level, higher mean stress goes together with stronger rule orientation and greater employment stability, and vice versa (p. 163). The actual computation of the uncertainty avoidance index uses mean percentage value for employment stability question and mean scores for the other two.

Hofstede has shown that there are high correlations between the three items used in each of the two indices across cultures. However, the correlation tests carried out between these items for the present data demonstrated low levels of inter-item association. Tables 6.7 and 6.8 give these correlations for the English and Indian samples, the pilot study, and the survey conducted by the author in Iran (Tayeb, 1979). The reason for the discrepancy between the results of Hofstede's tests and those of the present author's is that PDI and UAI are ecological measures and can be used only as characteristics of social systems, not of individuals (Hofstede, 1980: 103). According to Hofstede, comparisons between a small number of countries, say

Table 6.7 *Pearson correlation between core power distance items*

Surveys	a with b		a with c		b with c	
	coef.	p	coef.	p	coef.	p
Iranian	−0.05	0.34	0.43	0.001	−0.27	0.02
Pilot	0.15	0.14	0.09	0.25	−0.28	0.01
English	0.09	0.03	0.16	0.001	−0.07	0.08
Indian	−0.01	0.41	0.48	0.001	0.05	0.13

Note: a = perceived bosses.
b = employees afraid to disagree with their boss.
c = preferred boss.

Table 6.8 *Pearson correlation between core uncertainty avoidance items*

Surveys	a with b		a with c		b with c	
	coef.	p	coef.	p	coef.	p
Iranian	0.04	0.36	0.05	0.34	−0.29	0.01
Pilot	0.19	0.07	−0.10	0.22	−0.27	0.02
English	−0.09	0.04	0.13	0.008	−0.17	0.001
Indian	−0.008	0.44	0.06	0.12	−0.11	0.02

Note: a = tense or nervous at work.
b = breaking company rules.
c = how long continue to work with the company.

ten, will not easily show statistically significant correlations of ecological data. This means that these two indices are not valid instruments for use in small scale cross-cultural research.

Power distance and uncertainty avoidance have other drawbacks. Although they are meant to measure power distance and uncertainty avoidance as cultural dimensions, they are heavily influenced by non-cultural factors common to all modern civilized cultures, such as level of education, occupation, age and sex. Moreover, the effect of these non-cultural factors on the scales are not, at least as far as the findings of the present research demonstrate, consistent.

Power distance and non-cultural factors
Using Hofstede's formula, PDI for English and Indian samples in the present study was calculated. The two countries scored 70 and 67 respectively. In Hofstede's study, the British employees scored 35 and the Indian employees 77. However, the respondents in his study were middle managers; whereas the present samples consisted of employees of all levels from senior managers to shopfloor workers. This points, among other things, to the effect of the formal position of employees in an organization on their PDI. Table 6.9 was therefore constructed to compare the holders of different job categories in each sample with the colleagues in their own country as well as in the other country.

Table 6.9 *Power distance and occupation*

	English	Indian
1 Directors, and other managers	16	61
2 Superintendents, supervisors, foremen, section heads, etc	82	53
3 Technicians, engineers, inspectors, controllers, etc	49	70
4 Specialists, computer programmers, accountants, etc	52	70
5 Office workers, telephonists, etc	73	79
6 Manual workers	100	48

Note: The higher the score, the larger the power distance.

The PDI scores for different occupational categories are, as in Hofstede's study, different. However, he found that as one went lower down the hierarchy, the power distance increased. In the present study, in the English sample various occupational groups scored differently, but the differences are not systematic except for the highest (managers = 16) and the lowest (manual workers = 100) positions. In the Indian sample, supervisors and shopfloor employees (categories 2 and 6) scored lowest (smallest power distance). This is, perhaps, because the hierarchical position inside an organization per se is not enough, in the Indian sample at least, to explain the power distance perceived by the job holders. A political economy-type factor, that is, the 'protected' position of Indian manual workers, may have increased their sense of power. The respondents in categories 2 and 6 may hold lower-paid and lower-status jobs in their organization compared with other employees, but, thanks to the 'pro' workers' industrial legislation in India (see also Chapter 7), they may enjoy powers and privileges beyond the formal scope of their jobs. A comparison between the two samples further suggests that occupation plays a more important part in the PDI scores than cultural characteristics.

Education too is argued to be another factor which may influence PDI in such a way that an increase in the level of education will result in a decrease in power distance (p. 105). Table 6.10 illustrates the

Table 6.10 *Power distance and education*

	English	Indian
Masters	–*	69
University first degree	30	63
Training college	57	–*
'A' levels	67	79
'O' levels	78	66
Below 'O' levels	97	–*

Notes: * There were very few respondents in each of these categories and the number was too small to make PDI meaningful (see Table 8.3).

The higher the score, the larger the power distance.

PDI calculated for Indian and English employees grouped according to their level of education. As the table shows, in the English sample power distance decreases as the level of education goes up, but the pattern is not the same among the Indian respondents. This may be because of the nature of educational systems in the two countries. In the English educational system, teacher–pupil relationships, especially in universities and other institutions of higher education, are more egalitarian than is the case in the Indian system. The former helps reduce the power distance between authority positions; the latter helps maintain a large distance. However, in the Indian sample there is no systematic increase of power distance along with the increase in the level of education. PDI for 'A' level holders is higher than for the holders of a university first degree. Here the occupation of the respondents may have had more influence than education. A comparison between the educational groups across the two countries shows a confused and unsystematic picture.

The data collected in this part of the study also provide an opportunity to test the validity of PDI as a tool for measuring the combined influence of education and occupational status on power distance. Hofstede (p. 105) argues that lower-education, lower-status occupations tend to produce high PDI values and higher-education, higher-status occupations tend to produce low PDI values. If his argument is correct, and if PDI is capable of testing it, the following continuum should be the case for both samples:

low-educated manual workers	high-educated managers
large power distance	small power distance

In each sample, the manual workers holding 'O' levels or below were taken as low-education, low-status employees, and the managers with university degrees were taken as high-educated, high-status employees. The result of this exercise was as follows:

English sample:

low-educated manual workers	high-educated managers
100	30

Indian sample:

low-educated manual workers	high-educated managers
55	65

As the two continua show, the high-educated, English managers scored much lower on power distance compared to the low-educated manual workers in their country. In the Indian sample, however, high-educated managers scored higher than their less educated, lower status colleagues. Hofstede's argument is supported by the English data, but rejected by the Indian data. The explanation may be that either the association between power distance and the combined effect of education and occupational status is not as strong as Hofstede would argue, or the PDI cannot accurately measure the power distance between each of the above pairs of respondents.

The age of the respondents is another factor which is argued to influence the PDI value. Table 6.11 shows the PDI scores for dif-

Table 6.11 Power distance and age

	English	Indian
20 and under	84	–*
21–30	84	72
31–40	90	64
41–50	75	60
51–60	58	–*
60 and over	–*	–*

Note: * The number of respondents in these age groups was too small to make power distance scores meaningful (see Table 8.2).

ferent age groups in the two samples. In the Indian sample, as age increases, PDI score, in line with Hofstede's argument, increases, but in the English sample there is no such systematic relationship between age and power distance.

Uncertainty avoidance index and non-cultural factors

The speculated associations between UAI and non-cultural factors are also problematic. Here, the individual items comprising the scale, and not the scale itself, are assumed to be influenced by certain factors. The item related to stress and tension at work is argued to be affected by and correlated with occupation, and the item related to breaking company rules with level of education (p. 105). In the present study, in English data the correlation coefficient between education and rule orientation was -0.13 ($p = 0.008$), and between stress and occupation -0.003 ($p = 0.47$). In the Indian data, the coefficient was -0.06 ($p = 0.13$) in both cases. The correlations are very low indeed. Hofstede attributes this to the ecological nature of UAI. The fact that correlation and other statistical tests may yield meaningful patterns only when large number of countries are involved remains a major weakness of UAI, and PDI for that matter.

UAI has a problematic relationship with age too. Across *countries* age and UAI correlated at 0.52 in Hofstede's study. Further, age correlated separately with rule orientation (-0.45), with employment stability (-0.46) and with stress (-0.36). 'In order to test how strong the effect of age differences on the UAI country scores really

68 *Cultural and organizational assessment*

is', Hofstede (p. 193) offers the following formula of the regression line:

$$UAI = 7 \times (\text{average age in years}) - 157$$

'... which means that one year of increase in the average age of a country sample corresponds to a UAI increase of seven points' (p. 193).

In the present study, the average of the English sample was thirty-seven and of the Indian sample thirty-four. This means that, if the relationship between UAI and age is in the same manner as suggested by the above mentioned regression line, the UAI score for the English sample should be 102 and for the Indian sample 81. However, this is not the case. Using Hofstede's (p. 164) formula incorporating the UAI core items, the two samples scored 19 and 43 respectively – either UAI is not capable of measuring the respondents' degree of uncertainty avoidance or the connection between this dimension and age does not exist in the manner suggested by Hofstede.

Hofstede found that across *individuals* age was related to two of the three UAI questions. The correlation between age and stress was 0.90, between age and rule orientation -0.13 (older people more rule-oriented), and between age and employment stability -0.32 (older people more stable).

Table 6.12 was constructed to examine the pattern of correlation between age and UAI items for English and Indian samples. As can be seen, the pattern is somewhat different from that obtained in Hofstede's study. The limitations of the power distance and uncertainty avoidance indices make them unsuitable for use in cross-cultural studies, at least for those comparing a small number of countries.

Table 6.12 *Correlation between UAI items and age*

Samples	Stress		Rule orientation		Employment stability	
	r	p	r	p	r	p
English	0.10	0.03	-0.15	0.003	-0.54	0.001
Indian	0.009	0.43	0.06	0.12	-0.30	0.001
Hofstede's	0.00	1.00	-0.13	*	-0.32	**

Note: * $p < 0.05$, ** $p < 0.001$

ORGANIZATIONAL STRUCTURE SURVEY

The organizations

Fourteen organizations in England and the Indian State of Maharashtra were selected (seven companies in each country) which were matched in pairs across the two countries for their contextual variables. These variables were industry, product, production technology, size, status, ownership and control, age and market share. Because a perfect match on all these variables proved to be practically impossible, the level of control over certain factors, such as market share and age, had to be traded-off against control of others, such as size, technology and industry. For instance, two pharmaceutical companies were comparable on all contextual factors except age, and two computer companies were comparable on all except age and status. The trade-off was made on the basis of the importance and emphasis that other researchers have placed on these variables as predictors of structure. Moreover, the samples were chosen in such a way as to offer variations in terms of contextual factors within each country and thus enable the author to observe the effects of different contexts on structure. Table 8.1 in Chapter 8 shows the contextual variables of the organizations in comparison with their counterparts.

In order to decrease the complications in matching the two sets of organizations, the sample in each country was selected from among companies which (a) were engaged in manufacturing; (b) were profit-oriented; (c) operated in the private sector; and (d) were totally owned, managed and largely manned by people from their respective countries.

In order to compile the samples, various directories and relevant sources were consulted. In England a list of thirty selected companies was drawn from among 200 entries in *Kompass 1981*, *Key British Enterprises 1981*, and the 'Archive of the National Study' conducted by Child (1972b). The initial correspondence and preliminary meetings with the managing directors of these companies led to the selection of the seven English firms which were included in the study. For the Indian sample, an initial list of 295 companies in the relevant industries was prepared from among the entries in *The Times of India Directory 1980–1981* and *Kothari's Economic and Industrial Guide of India 1981*. The initial correspondence with the chief executives of these companies reduced the number of organizations comparable to the English sample to eighteen. After a preliminary meeting with each of the senior managers in India, the most appropriate seven firms were selected, within which the Indian study was conducted.

The interview schedule and scales

The interview schedule had six sections which covered the items related to contextual and structural variables.

The industries in which the fourteen organizations were engaged were brewery, confectionery and soft drinks, chemicals, pharmaceuticals (one pair in each), and electronics (three pairs).

In each organization the product or a group of very similar products which accounted for over 50 percent of its turnover was considered as the main product. The degree of change in dominant technology was measured using information about the following matters: (1) frequency of change in manufacturing technology; (2) frequency of change in product technology; (3) frequency of introduction of modified products and change in the ingredients; (4) frequency of introduction of a brand new product or design; and (5) the percentage of annual turnover spent on R & D. In the case of the first four items, a five-point answer scale ranging from 'little or none' to 'continuously' and in the case of R & D expenditure the absolute figures were used in the measurement of technological change.

The status measure distinguished between an independent organization with production unit(s), an independent organization without production unit(s), and a wholly-owned autonomous subsidiary. Four categories of ownership were used to classify the fourteen organizations: (1) a family; (2) private shareholders; (3) general public shareholders; and (4) a parent group. The control variable distinguished between (1) members of a family; (2) members of a family and salaried managers; (3) owner chairman and salaried managers; and (4) salaried managers. The levels at which the assessment was made were chairman, managing director/chief executive, and board of directors.

The market share variable was the share of the organization in the main product market as estimated by its managing directors. Also six items were included in the interview schedule to determine the nature of the competition that the organization faced. Size was measured in terms of the number of full-time employees and age was a count of the number of years since the organization was first established.

The main structural parameters studied were centralization, formalization, functional specialization, chief executive's span of control, height, communication pattern, control system, and reward and punishment policies. The working definitions and scales measuring the first five dimensions were adopted from the Abbreviated Aston Schedule (Inkson et al., 1970) with some modifications.

The centralization scale consisted of items covering financial, operative, marketing and other strategic decisions. As a modification to the original scale, ten new items were included to cover more decision areas. Also, financial items distinguished between allocated and unallocated expenditure. Each category was broken down to smaller sections, ranging from less than £50 to above £20,000 – making a scale with sixty items in all. The centralization dimension was computed using the Aston six-point scale ranging from 'above chief executive = 5', to 'operator = 0'.

In addition, a delegation score for each organization was computed using the answers to the centralization items to determine the degree to which the chief executive delegated authority down the hierarchy. The score for each decision was computed by a count of the number of levels down from the chief executive to the level at which the decision was taken. The sum of the scores for all decisions made up the total delegation score for the organization.

In the Aston Programme procedures, where a decision is made in collaboration by two or more people, the score for each item would be determined by the position of the senior partner in each case. However, this missed the point that in some organizations more decisions were made jointly than others. A new scale, which may be called 'joint decisions', was computed on the basis of the number of decisions made in each organization described by the interviewee as 'in conjunction with . . .', 'in consultation with . . .', 'jointly with . . .', and the like.

The centralization score, although it says something about the degree of centralization of the decision-making process in an organization, does not reveal anything about the power that the employees perceive themselves to have and their involvement in decision making, mainly because the scale is based on the information given by the senior managers who participate in the interview programme. In order to gain further insight into the decision-making process in these organizations and how the employees perceived it, five questions were included in the attitudes survey questionnaire administered in the second stage of the study. These items, which may collectively be called 'perceived autonomy', were adopted from Aiken and Hage (1968) and Hage and Aiken 1969) (see Table 8.7 in Chapter 8).

The formalization scale consisted of nineteen items and measured the extent to which written rules, procedures, and instructions were used to define roles and describe jobs. The functional specialization section consisted of nineteen items covering activities that could potentially be carried out by specialists. Three items in the scale were new and were concerned with policy making, strategic planning and information processing. The chief executive's span of control was a count of the people who reported directly to him. Height was a count of the levels in the main production hierarchy between chief executive and direct workers, inclusive of both.

The communication pattern section measured the degree to which vertical and lateral communication and consultation took place within the organization and between the organization and people from outside. The pattern was determined on the basis of the amount of time spent by employees with (1) their boss; (2) their subordinates; (3) their colleagues; (4) people from other areas/sections in the organization; and (5) people from outside the organization. Five items corresponding to these communication channels were included in the attitudes survey questionnaire which was administered in the second stage of the study.

The section on control strategies, reward and punishment policies was based on three main questions around which discussion and further ad hoc questions evolved.

Information about organizational structures and contexts was collected through an interview programme conducted in English in both countries. The main participant in each company was the managing director (or his equivalent). In almost all the firms other senior managers, such as technical director, finance director, sales/ marketing director and manufacturing/production manager, were also interviewed to obtain complementary information. On average, three senior managers in each organization were formally interviewed. The interviews were complemented by company documents and informal discussions and meetings.

The study was piloted both in England and India. The main English study was carried out between September 1981 and May 1982 and the Indian study in February and March 1983.

Finally, some discussion is necessary of the sample size used in the present study. The importance of obtaining relatively large samples of data in field surveys rests on the need to guard against the risk of detecting spurious differences between populations where sampling strategy cannot be precisely controlled. In this study the alternative strategy of tightly controlling the nature of the firms comprising the sampling frame was used. By controlling the eight aspects of the organizations sampled, it was expected that the risk of spuriously detecting differences between English and Indian samples would be controlled. Whether or not this was in fact accomplished must ultimately be judged in terms of whether the differences which are actually found are coherently explicable in terms of known aspects of the two cultures, or whether they are more plausibly seen as random error. Chapters 7, 8 and 9 will discuss the findings of the three stages of the fieldwork. (The questionnaires and interview schedule employed in the surveys are reproduced in Tayeb, 1984, and are available from the author.)

7
England and India as Social and Cultural Settings for Organizations

England is a part of the United Kingdom of Great Britain and Northern Ireland and is located in the northern hemisphere, off the main land of the continent of Europe. It emerged in recorded history with the arrival of the Celts in the British Isles. It was occupied by the Romans in the first century AD; their withdrawal in the fifth century was followed by a series of raids and settlements by Angles, Saxons, Jutes, Vikings and Normans, up to the eleventh century.

Immigration from Europe over the centuries has led to the establishment of Irish and Jewish communities in many of the larger cities. In the latter part of the twentieth century immigrants from the South Asian countries and the Caribbean also formed distinctive urban communities.

The total population of England is over 46 million. At the time the fieldwork for the English part of the present study was being carried out, on average 10.5 percent of the economically active people in England and Wales were unemployed. The unemployment rate varied in different parts of the country. The highest rate was 25 percent in Merseyside and the inner areas of Birmingham, and the lowest 4.1 percent in East Surrey.

India is located in the northern hemisphere and is a part of the continent of Asia. The origins of the Indian culture have been traced back to a pre-Arian civilization that lasted from 2500 to 1500 BC. The country as a whole or in parts has been periodically invaded and ruled by the Persians, Monguls, French, Portuguese and other peoples. The last colonial power was the British Raj whose rule lasted about 200 years and was ended in 1947 with the Declaration of Independence.

India, a union of states, consists of twenty-two states and nine union territories. Under the Constitution, the areas of jurisdiction of the union and states are demarcated. The states have their own assemblies and council of ministers as well as being represented in the union legislature, the Parliament, in the capital. The total population of the country is around 800 millions, of which almost 75 percent live in rural areas.

PRIMARY AND SECONDARY SOCIAL INSTITUTIONS

Family

English middle-class and working-class families
The present middle-class family in England is nuclear and loosely knit. Many writers suggest that this system is one of the consequences of changes which occurred in the eighteenth and nineteenth centuries following the Industrial Revolution. Macfarlane (1978), however, traces the origins of individualistic and loosely-knit family structure in England as far back as the early thirteenth century.

Contemporary middle-class families are generally egalitarian partnerships where wives have the same freedom as their husbands, responsibilities are shared, and the distinctions between the husband's and wife's familial tasks are blurred (Farmer, 1970). However, not all the middle-class families either live up to or accept the ideal of equal, mutually shared responsibilities between the marriage partners.

Children in the middle-class families are regarded as independent individuals and their privacy is respected. They are 'pushed' towards independence at an early age. After the age of puberty, children have great freedom in such matters as further education, marriage, social intercourse, and occupation, but parents may very subtly and indirectly influence their choices in these matters.

Child-rearing practices in the middle-class families are developmental and directed towards the encouragement of the cognitive processes of reasoning, planning, imagination and self-control, and are of the kind that Klein (1965) calls the 'problem-solving approach'. Some of the consequences for a child reared in this way are independence of the group, tolerance for ambiguity, ability to face reality with little strain, and ability to act independently of adult affection and attention (Radke, 1946; Klein, 1965). Emphasis on success and achievement dominates child rearing in middle-class families. High standards of performance are expected of the child, success is rewarded and failure punished (Raynor, 1969).

Discipline is another aspect of child-rearing practices which is greatly emphasized in English middle-class families, and there is sometimes punishment of undesirable traits as well as reward for good behaviour. The punishments more generally used are some sort of deprivation: withdrawing privileges, forbidding or withdrawing favourite toys or pastimes, and temporarily stopping pocket money (Gorer, 1955; Klein, 1965). Farmer (1970) argues that these methods of discipline are guilt producing, and they develop a strict conscience, which in the end leads the child to discipline himself, irrespective of the presence of an authority figure, be it parent, teacher or policeman. These methods give the child an awareness of the feelings of others, and the capacity to face up to difficulties and to cope with them.

The English working-class family is a network of closely-knit and dense relationships, and privacy is less readily available. The family structure is characterized to a large degree by a strict role and task allocation between sexes. The ideal wife is patient, submissive, home-centred and self-effacing as regards her husband's interests. This, however, may be less the case in the younger generation of working-class families.

Life for the working-class child on the whole is harsher than that of his middle-class counterpart and he is more likely to receive corporal punishment as a form of discipline. Reward when it is used is also direct and tangible: treats, rather than approval. Attitudes are more authoritarian: father is the head of the household and demands obedience from the child. Children's independence is, however, valued (Rose, 1968; Roberts, 1978).

Indian family
While there are obvious differences between one family and another, their similarities are more striking and more significant (Lannoy, 1971).

A distinctive feature of Indian society is the joint family. Traditionally this type of family, which originated in Vedic times, was patriarchal: the oldest male member was absolute head, under whose roof his younger brothers and their families, his sons and their wives and children, and his grandchildren all lived. Members were related by an interlocking pattern of mutual dependence. Individuality was subordinate to collective solidarity, and the younger generation was strictly controlled by the elders (Lannoy, 1971). In the face of the economic and social changes which Indian society has undergone, the joint family has not disintegrated but has adapted itself to the modern industrial setting and continues functionally to be the same. As Ramu (1981) states, although the joint family may no longer exist in the 'physical' sense, it continues to do so in 'spirit'.

The author's observations and experience with Indian families and the literature indicate that a joint family, physical or spiritual, may have certain consequences for its members. The most significant of these are (a) little or no privacy for individuals; (b) close emotional relationships and mutual dependence; (c) conformity; (d) little or no opportunity for individuals, especially the younger ones, to exercise initiative, independence and pursuit of personal goals which are in conflict with the interests of the family as a whole; (e) psychological and economic security and stability; and (f) continuity of traditional values and culture.

The husband and wife relationship, especially in arranged marriages, which constitute almost all marriages in India, is not based on love but on matrimonial duties. The husband's love and loyalty are primarily for his parental family, and the wife seeks the outlet for her love and emotions in her sons (my own observations; Segal, 1971). The woman's position in the family is generally inferior to that of her husband, and she is on the whole regarded as his possession and expected to be obedient and submissive. The media reports abound with incidents of the harassment and subjugation of wives by their husbands and in-laws (e.g. 'Wheels of Fire', BBC broadcast, 11 August 1983).

The position of the father in relation to the children is generally that of an authority figure with indisputable power and control. The position of the mother is one of tender love and care. There is a strong emotional bond between parents and children. Parents usually, in the words of one of many Indians with whom I discussed the subject, 'in the absence of any other creative activity in an ordinary person's life, regard their children as their own creation and as such they love them, possess them and dominate them'. Children, especially in the better-off families, are both emotionally and economically dependent on their parents until late in life. Many major and minor decisions related to the children's affairs, such as type of schooling, choice of the subjects to study at college and university, marriage partner, job, purchase of a house, are taken by parents and other elder members of the family. The children are very directly and openly assisted in whatever they do, such as school homework, changing clothes, and in some cases these are done for them. This type of familial relationship tends to make children rather dependent on their parents' advice and instructions in whatever they wish to do. However, in poor families, where both parents and even children themselves have to work, the parents do not have as much time to spend on the children who have to learn to look after themselves and their younger siblings, and to stand on their own feet at an early age.

Discipline in an Indian family generally takes a direct and physical form, but other means, such as a threat of withdrawal of love, are also employed. Usually, the children in better-off families are more pampered and less disciplined compared to their poorer counterparts. Boys are 'spoiled' more than girls. However, in educational matters, such as school homework, and respect for seniors, discipline is very harsh, especially for boys. Almost all the Indian men with whom I discussed their childhood experiences said they were frequently beaten by their fathers.

Ambitions and goals set for children by their parents, depending on their social standing, are success in education, a well-paid job, marriage and setting up a home. The children are constantly 'pushed' towards achieving these goals and towards aiming as high as possible. The children's achievement, and for that matter the achievement of any other member of the family and close relatives, is the achievement of the family as a whole – a typical characteristic of a collectivist culture.

Religion

Religion of the English

The main religion of the English is Christianity, especially Protestant and Roman Catholic denominations. However, Rowntree and Lavers wrote in 1951 that a majority of the population had rejected so much of the Christian story as related in the New Testament that no church would recognize them as Christians at all. Gorer (1955), in a seminal survey of 'English character', found that one quarter of the population of England did not consider they belonged to any religion or denomination. However, there appears to be a substantial measure of practical Christianity in the way people deal with each other, the standards of right and wrong, and what the pattern of life should be (Rowntree and Lavers, 1951). On the whole, women seem to be more religious than men, the old than the young, and the upper than the lower social strata (Gorer, 1955; Martin, 1967).

A vast majority of those who claim any church membership belong to some organized Protestant Church, especially the Church of England. Protestantism was initiated by Luther in Germany in the early sixteenth century and expanded by Calvin in Switzerland. It came to England during the reign of Henry VIII.

Weber (1930) argued that the change of the economic structure in England from feudalism to capitalism and private ownership occurred in the sixteenth century. One of the contributory factors to this change was the peculiar 'ethic' which stressed untiring, never-ending acquisition which developed in certain parts of Protestant Europe. In Weber's view, Protestantism stood at the cradle of the modern economic person, and Calvinism in particular stressed the individual, one's own ability and initiative. Thus, although modern capitalism 'was derived from the peculiarities of the social structure of Occident, it was inconceivable without Calvinism' (p. 25), for it 'had the psychological effect of freeing the acquisition of goods from the inhibitions of traditionalistic ethics' (p. 171).

Christianity, according to Weber (Benedix, 1966), was one of the factors which broke the original 'clan' system in Europe. It encouraged an abstract, non-familistic attitude, and stressed individual behaviour; every Christian community was basically a confessional association of individual believers, not a ritual association of kinship groups, and Protestantism was especially powerful in its attack on the 'fetters' of earlier kinship systems.

It seems, however, that the origins of individualism and the 'capitalist ethic' in England lay well before the sixteenth century. Macfarlane (1978) argues that 'the majority of people in England from at least the thirteenth century were rampant individualists, highly mobile both geographically and socially, economically "rational", market-oriented and acquisitive, and ego-centred in kinship and social life' (p. 163), and from the thirteenth century onward 'it is not possible to find a time when an Englishman did not stand alone. Symbolized and shaped by his ego-centred kinship system, he stood in the centre of his world' (p. 196).

Since its adoption by the English, Protestantism appears to have encouraged and reinforced individualism and the spirit of capitalism. This spirit, which once was the major driving force behind the Industrial Revolution, seems to have declined among the English during this century (Barnett, 1972; Roderick and Stephenson, 1978, 1981, 1982; Wiener, 1981).

The religion of the Indians
The main religion in India is Hinduism. The 1981 general census shows that 82.7 percent of the population are Hindus, 11.2 percent Muslims, and the rest are mainly Christians, Sikhs, Zoroastrians, Buddhists and Jains. The majority of people are very religious, even superstitious, and perform religious functions and rituals on a daily basis as well as on special occasions. On the whole Indian women seem to be more religious than men, and rural people more so than the educated urban population. However, education and occupation among the latter do not appear to have fundamentally changed their religious beliefs and values. The author met a Cambridge-educated senior government official who believed his rise in the professional and social life was owed as much to his daughter's prayers as to his qualifications and efforts. Also, one frequently came across educated young men and women who wore 'lucky' stones on their necklace and rings and regularly consulted fortune-tellers and astrologers.

The main characteristic of Hinduism is a belief in a stratified social structure where people are placed, by birth, in certain hierarchically ordered exclusive categories of castes. There are four castes or *varnas* to each of which thousands of sub-castes and sub-sub-castes or *jatis* belong. These castes are, in descending order in terms of purity and social status, *Brahmin* (priests), *Kshatriya* (warriors, aristocrats), *Vaisa* (traders, merchants), and *Sudra* (cultivators, servants). The *Harijans* (Untouchables) are generally regarded as outcastes and do not fall into any of the four *varsas*.

In the day-to-day life, especially in urban areas, one does not notice the existence of caste as a barrier to communication and socialization between people, but in matters such as marriage caste is a serious consideration. Movements from lower castes and sub-castes to higher ones are possible, but, as Beteille (1969) notes, it may take generations of following the life style of a particular caste or sub-caste.

Hinduism, like many other religions, is ambivalent on the question of free will and fatalism. This is mingled with the belief in reincarnation (cycle of rebirths). On the one hand, humans are born into their *jati* and have to suffer or enjoy their predicament, depending on their deeds in their previous lives, a predicament from which there is no escape in this life. However, on the other hand, humans can improve their plight in the next life, in terms of being born into a higher *jati* and caste, by good deeds in this life, and eventually uniting with God and ridding themselves of the misery of rebirth. It seems that, as far as this life is concerned, Hinduism is a fatalist creed. But it recognizes free will for humans as far as their future life cycles are concerned.

Other basic precepts of Hinduism are an emphasis on self-control, self-renunciation and spiritualism, yet encouragement of material success, role differentiation between man and woman, observance of rules of purity and avoidance of pollution, and tolerance of others' religious beliefs. However, the last point, according to *The Gentleman* (21 May 1983) is no longer the case among contemporary Indians. The frequent violent clashes between religious groups in various parts of the country are evidence to this remark.

Education

Education in England
Education in modern England is a large-scale activity. Virtually all adult members of the English society have experienced nine or more years of full-time formal education. The aspects of the English educational system which are of particular relevance to the present study are teaching practices, values, and priorities.

Modern teaching practices in England are based on the traditions enriched by theories advocated by many eighteenth- and nineteenth-century writers, such as Rousseau, Owen, Spencer, and practitioners, such as Arnold and Butler (Barnard, 1961). The essence of these theories is that (a) education should be regarded as development and cultivation of the possibilities native to the human being, based on observation, self-discovery, and experience by the pupil; (b) emphasis must be put on the methods which stimulate self-activity, self-reliance and self-experience in intellectual and moral matters; (c) the child should not be given a rule, but should be led to make her own investigation and generalization from the particulars which she observes; and (d) play is an important part of education, as it encourages the child's natural development.

The values and culture of the English educational system are more closely related to the culture of middle-class than to that of the working-class people. The emphasis is on activities related to success, ambition, individuality, resourcefulness, control of aggression, respect for property and postponement of immediate satisfaction in the interest of long-term achievement (Sugarman, 1966; Hargreaves, 1967; King, 1977).

A major feature of the English educational system is its emphasis on arts and classics and a relatively low priority for engineering and technology. This, according to many writers, has contributed to the industrial decline of the country in this century (e.g. Wiener, 1981; Jenkins, 1982; Lorenz, 1982).

A major vehicle through which the middle-class values are percolated down the educational system are the public schools. These schools, which are exclusively private, were originally set up in the fourteenth and fifteenth centuries under the Church and royal patronage for 'poor scholars'. By the mid-eighteenth century the schools were completely taken over by the sons of the aristocracy and gentry.

The influence of public schools on the value system is exerted through two channels. First, they are models for the state schools. Secondly, the graduates of the public schools occupy the majority of the positions of power and persuasion and prestige in business and public life (Sampson, 1982a, 1982b).

Much of the organization of the public schools relates to their total character. Pupils are subject to a formal round of life under fairly constant supervision. The smooth running of the schools puts a premium on conformity, loyalty, acceptance of authority and concealment of emotions (King, 1977). However, the schools also claim to encourage 'individualistic' traits via an emphasis on leadership and hobbies. Yet this is a qualified individualism confined to strict socially acceptable limits and incorporated into the wider notion of the 'team', which in adult life becomes the 'social élite'.

Education in India

According to the 1981 census, only 36.17 percent of the total population of India are literate. Formal education, unlike family and religion, does not play a significant part in the upbringing of the majority of Indians.

There are four types of schools in India: the English-style public schools, independent private schools, state run and controlled schools, and centre schools whose curricula and administration come under the central government authority. The first two categories care for the children of a very small élite and constitute a negligible percentage of all the schools in the country. They usually provide the students with a variety of means of learning, ranging from laboratories, to libraries, games and sporting facilities. For the remaining schools, their only means for transmitting learning, apart from lectures given by teachers, are textbooks whose publication and contents are controlled by the state or central governments. Pupils are forced to memorize 'facts', which are more often than not 'out-dated' and 'full of mistakes' (*The Times of India*, 27 March 1983: 4) and reproduce them in examinations. These books are generally written or compiled by 'incompetent and unimaginative – and at times even unscrupulous – authors ... Genuinely qualified people do not write textbooks; they regard it as below their dignity to write for school children or even undergraduates' (p. 1).

Textbooks have been primarily responsible for killing the interest of young minds in learning. Indian education, as the leader comments of *The Times of India* put it, is nothing but 'sheep-herding', where all the student knows 'is to recite marked portions in his or her textbooks' (p. 1). There is, therefore, no scope for innovation. 'They begin to believe that everything in black-and-white is the gospel truth and make no effort to find out things for themselves' (p. 1).

Another major characteristic of the system is the emphasis on conformity. One brilliant child, the *Indian Express Sunday Magazine* (10 April 1983: 2) reports, had an entire essay crossed through with the remark 'not in text'. The system does not seem to encourage creativity, self-discovery, curiosity, divergent opinions, self-expression and reading books other than those related to school books.

A third major characteristic of the educational system is its tradition-oriented policies. As the commentator of the *Indian Express Sunday Magazine* argues, 'In India, we have a tradition-oriented educational policy, with examinations, grading, strict dress conformity, punishment for originality and rigorous homework requirements from kindergarten upwards' (p. 2). The emphasis is on learning for certificates and degrees and not on development of the mind (p. 2).

Political system

English political system
The political system is based on the principle of parliamentary democracy and party government. The head of the state is the Crown, a legal concept of office, not the monarch in person. Most of the Crown's constitutional powers are in practice exercised by the government in the name of the Crown and the monarch must nearly always act on advice, not personal initiative.

Parliament consists of a 'House of Commons' whose members are elected by British people and the citizens of other Commonwealth countries, and an upper house, the 'House of Lords', whose members are hereditary and life peers, bishops and archbishops, and who are not elected by the electorate.

In terms of power, Parliament's part in making policy is very circumscribed and its chief function is to watch the government critically and ask questions. The cabinet occupies a central and dominant position in the system, and decides policies and devises tactics. It has been argued by academics and politicians alike (e.g. Benn, 1982; Hunt, 1982) that the Prime Minister is now undoubtedly the most powerful member of the government.

The present political culture reflects a range of attitudes and is the product of a long process of historical development. In the words of Beer (1982), political culture of the past two decades represents the following sets of values and attitudes: Tory values whose direction would seem to be towards a corporatist economy, managed by a technocratic élite, and moderated by the traditional controls of party government and parliamentary democracy. The neo-liberals, Mrs Thatcher and her followers, who seek to move the burdens of social choice from government and politics to the market. A Bevenite version of socialism, based on a centralized bureaucratic state, would tend towards a planned economy, with egalitarian social programmes enjoying the support of a coherent trade union movement and of a mass party of 'workers by hand and brain'. Neo-socialism, its principal advocate being Tony Benn, departs sharply from Bevenite collectivism in its thrust towards a radical decentralization and democratization of the economy. The neo-radicals, including mainly the Liberals and the Social Democrats, in economic and social policy eschew a drastic move from the middle ground, and they take their stand to the left of centre.

The major political parties who represent these values are Conservative (Tory), Labour, Liberal and Social Democratic parties. In the past sixty years or so governments have been formed either by the Conservative or Labour parties. Traditionally, the Conservatives find their support chiefly in rural areas and in the southern half of the country, while the Labour Party derives its main support from the urban industrialized areas, especially in the northern half of the country.

Pressure groups, such as the Campaign for Nuclear Disarmament, and ad hoc groups who organize themselves to try to prevent government authorities taking certain actions, exercise their influence and pressure from outside Parliament through bargaining with ministers and senior civil servants, and lobbying members of Parliament. Through membership of pressure groups individual English men and women indirectly participate in the making of public policies.

Newspapers and other mass media are other channels through which information and opinions pass between politicians and the electorate. The government itself does not own any newspaper, and no broadcasting station is directly controlled by it. However, the government on occasion does exercise influence over the broadcasting of politically 'sensitive' issues, such as some matters relating to Northern Ireland and IRA activities, the handling of news about the Falkland Islands crisis while it lasted (*Panorama*, BBC broadcast, 18 October 1982), and the BBC documentary series *Secret Society*, where government authorities advise the media to hold back, thereby controlling and censoring information to be given to the public. The government in recent times has sought to use the Official Secrets Act to reduce the flow of information available to the public.

Indian political system
The government of India is based on parliamentary democracy, with a president as the executive head. On paper the president enjoys enormous authority, but in practice he or she acts on the advice of the Council of Ministers through the Prime Minister. The Parliament consists of two chambers: the Lok Sabha (House of People) whose members are directly elected by people, and the Rajya Sabha (Council of States), some of whose members are nominated by the President and the others are elected by the legislative assemblies of the states and union territories.

Indian democracy has certain characteristics which make it very different from many other democracies, especially those in Western societies. First, the government machinery is very centralized and the Centre has far more substantial powers in relation to the states than exists in any other similar federation (Segal, 1971). For instance, the central government can declare a state of emergency, not only in times of war but even to maintain law and order and proper government in the states, and it can assume extraordinary powers over constituent states and over individual citizens whose fundamental rights may be disregarded.

Secondly, the opposition is fragmented into many small groups, none of which qualifies for recognition as a distinct political party because none has the requisite 10 percent of the seats in Parliament (*Financial Times*, 24 May 1983). Since Independence, virtually only one party, the Congress Party, has been in power. This dominance of the Congress Party over the political scene has resulted in an almost single-party system and the electorate is not given a meaningful national choice.

Thirdly, because of the dominance of the government by the Congress Party, at the time of elections, Congress politicians make extensive use of government facilities and officials to organize their campaigns and this gives them an enormous advantage compared to their financially and otherwise weaker rival candidates (Segal, 1971).

Fourthly, the elections are in most cases far from free and fair. Party workers usually spend a lot of money and organize lunch and dinner sessions for villagers or distribute food items among them to induce them to vote for their candidates. There are also cases of violation of rules and fraud (see, for instance, the article by Rajinder Puri, the political editor of the *Sunday Observer*, 20 March 1983: 6, about state elections in Assam).

The political culture of India today covers a range of viewpoints represented by various parties. In the words of Sharma, a commentator of the *Financial Times* (24 May 1982), 'the Congress follows a Gandhian (after the Mahatma) socialist policy but is pragmatic in its beliefs'. For instance, the Congress government has in the past pursued a right-wing economic policy while at the same time accepting overtures from the Communists. The Communist Party (Marxist) and the Communist Party of India draw their inspiration from Russia. The Janata Party follows a vague Gandhian policy but has no distinct ideology. The Lok Dal (People's Party) represents the interests of the high-caste farmers in northern states. The Bharatya Janata Party is essentially the representative of the urban orthodox Hindus, with a hankering for what it thinks is a true Indian culture.

All India Radio and Doordarshan (television network) are directly run, controlled and manipulated by the government. As a result, instead of playing a neutral role, these media act as 'government mouthpieces' (the *Statesman*, 23 April 1983). The censorship of the news is to the extent that, as a reader of the *Statesman* puts it, 'people need to tune to the BBC and Voice of America to know what is happening in their own country' (p. 6).

Newspapers, however, enjoy freedom of expression, and criticize government bodies, politicians and other public figures freely. The

Indian press, unlike radio and television, is not a monolithic body, and represents a wide range of social and political values and views. Indeed, India has been claimed to be the only society outside the Western world where issues of public importance can still be debated freely in the press (*India Today*, 31 March 1983).

Socio-economic structure

English economic system
England was the home of capitalism and it determined the evolution of capitalism (Weber, 1930, 1961). The capitalist system developed slowly in England. At the end of the Middle Ages there was a system that could be called 'commercial capitalism'. This system changed to the 'industrial capitalism' in the eighteenth century and for nearly 200 years was of a *laissez faire* nature, which implied opposition to government interference and a belief in free competition and unrestricted liberty of the individual (Dore, 1973; Macfarlane, 1978).

The contemporary economy can hardly be called a pure version of capitalism since it is characterized by a mixture of freedom and control, and of private and state enterprises. The emphasis on freedom or control shifts from time to time depending on the policies of the government of the day. Since the 1920s, Labour governments have tended to use direct powers to control the economy, in addition to using fiscal measures to regulate growth. Conservative governments, on the other hand, have tended to rely mainly on fiscal policy, or 'monetarism', rather than direct intervention.

The policies of the present Conservative government, which has been in power since 1979, are based on minimal government intervention, and stimulating industry through monetary policies which aim at facilitating the free play and interaction of market forces. In the pursuit of this aim, there is very little control over imports and, as a result, manufacturing companies face fierce competition from foreign firms.

Indian economic system
Although India has become an industrial power in its own right (ninth in the world), agriculture is still the mainstay of its economy – it is by far the largest single employer in the country and accounts for around 40 percent of the country's gross national product (*Financial Times*, 24 March 1982).

India's economy may be described as mixed, with protective interventionist policies, where the private sector is allowed to operate under governmental guidelines and direct control, and where the government also owns and manages manufacturing and service industries. Like many other third world countries, the government's objectives in economic planning are mainly: removal of poverty, creation of employment, attainment of self-reliance, reduction of inequalities in income and wealth (through high taxes and a low upper limit for wages and salaries), and attainment of balanced regional developments. The government tries to achieve these goals by exerting its hold over the economy through such means as carrying out five-year economic plans, issuing licences for setting up factories, discriminative licensing policies for different industries according to the country's needs, giving priority to applicants who set up factories in the 'centrally noted backward areas', strict import control to protect domestic industries, restricting establishment and expansion of capital intensive high technology industries, and setting up social goals, such as employment and prosperity of backward areas, before profit for private industries (Mehta, 1982). Although in the past few years government has eased its hold on the economy, especially the private sector, and relaxed its import policies, the economic policy is still highly protectionist and far from being based on a free market (*The Guardian*, 23 March 1982; *Financial Times*, 16 June 1982, 26 January 1983, 24 May 1983; *India Today*, 15 June 1983).

English trade unions
Although the origins of the trade union movement can be traced back to the craft guilds of the Middle Ages, the modern trade union is essentially a product of the Industrial Revolution (Irwin, 1976). Union membership is industry and craft based and cuts across firms and organizations. Gallie (1978) found that English unions see their role as one of representing the workforce, that is, pushing for objectives that are consciously desired by the workers themselves. Unlike trade unions in some other European countries, such as Poland and France, the English unions are more pragmatic in their approach and fight for better pay settlements and working conditions within the present economic and social system rather than engaging in class struggle and ideological battles for the overthrow of the system. Since the establishment of the Labour Party in 1906, which grew out of the trade union movement, they have been able to use it to further their interests as well as being its major source of finance. In recent years, under the present Conservative Government, much of the power of trade unions has been eroded. The decline in membership due to mass redundancies caused by economic recession and the introduction of new technology, and the anti-union legislation of the government (for example, the banning of secondary picketing and the ending of the closed-shop practice) have been suggested as some of the reasons for the loss of the trade unions' power (Bain, 1983; *The*

Social and cultural settings 87

Times, 2 September 1983; 'International Assignment', BBC Radio 4, 2 December 1983).

Indian trade unions
There are no craft unions in India. Trade unions are either plant based or national organizations which are run locally in each state and focus their activities on the interest of their immediate members at the plant or local industry level. There are provisions for setting up works committees in factories and workers' participation in decision making at shopfloor and plant level. However, these committees, and indeed any other form of workers' participation, have not been successful (Chauduri, 1981). There are various acts of Parliament which secure minimum wages, regulation for payment of wages, working conditions, equal remuneration for men and women, and several schemes providing security to the workers against contingencies, such as industrial accidents. Generally, industrial relations legislation is pro-worker and aims at protecting their employment and general well-being. For instance, the regulations are such that it is virtually impossible for management to sack a worker or reduce her wages even if she has seriously breached the terms of her contract. All of India's ten central trade union organizations are committed to political parties. In the past few years the unions have found themselves being increasingly used as a weapon, or convenience, by their political affiliates. The nationwide railway strike in 1974 and the two-year-old textile strike in Bombay in 1983 are examples of this kind.

English social structure
The social structure of modern England is described as stratified. The stratification is based primarily on economic factors such as occupation, wealth and ownership and/or control of means of production. On this basis, the society is divided into two large middle and working classes, with a relatively small 'upper' class and 'under' class of low-paid women and the unemployed at either end of the social hierarchy. Class membership in England has a 'subjective' aspect, and the system is dynamic and flexible, with the opportunity for movement from one class to another. For instance, a former member of the working class can consider himself a member of the middle class once his occupation and economic conditions change from a working-class category and type (manual work) to a middle-class category and type (for example, managerial work).

Indian social structure
Indian people are not so much class conscious as conscious of their caste and sub-castes. The society is still stratified on the basis of caste

Table 7.1 English character

Characteristic	Agreement (percentage)	Characteristic	Agreement (percentage)
1 Interested in community affairs	57.0	7 Cope well with set-backs	77.8
Indifferent to community affairs	18.0	Do not cope well with set-backs	9.1
A mix of the two	25.0	A mix of the two	13.1
2 Honest	75.8	8 Rational	57.7
Dishonest	8.1	Irrational	19.5
A mix of the two	16.2	A mix of the two	22.7
3 Modest	35.4	9 Independent of their parents	70.4
Arrogant	34.3	Dependent on their parents	13.3
A mix of the two	30.3	A mix of the two	16.3
4 Respect the law to the letter	48.5	10 Reserved	43.9
Prepared to bend the law	25.2	Out-going	27.5
A mix of the two	26.3	A mix of the two	28.6
5 Self-confident	71.4	11 Aggressive	45.0
Lack self-confidence	8.2	Submissive	18.0
A mix of the two	20.4	A mix of the two	37.0
6 Have trust in others	58.0	12 Law abiding	70.0
Do not trust others	20.0	Law breaking	12.0
A mix of the two	22.0	A mix of the two	18.0

Table 7.1 *English character* (continued)

Characteristic	Agreement (percentage)	Characteristic	Agreement (percentage)
13 Believe in sharing fairly	48.0	19 Respect powerful people	44.0
Selfish	25.5	Do not respect powerful people	27.0
A mix of the two	26.5	A mix of the two	29.0
14 Obedient to their seniors	61.0	20 Willing to take account of others' opinions	38.0
Disobedient to their seniors	18.0	Prefer to impose their own opinion on others	33.0
A mix of the two	21.0	A mix of the two	29.0
15 Opposed to change	42.0	21 Have a strong sense of responsibility	80.0
Accept change	41.0	Have no sense of responsibility	6.0
A mix of the two	17.0	A mix of the two	14.0
16 Trustworthy	79.8	22 Play safe	37.4
Not trustworthy	7.1	Take chances	35.4
A mix of the two	13.1	A mix of the two	27.3
17 Unemotional	31.0	23 Not afraid of powerful people	64.0
Emotional	31.0	Afraid of powerful people	21.0
A mix of the two	38.0	A mix of the two	15.0
18 Disciplined	67.0	24 Do not believe in fate	29.3
Undisciplined	10.0	Believe in fate	28.3
A mix of the two	23.0	A mix of the two	42.4

Table 7.1 English character (continued)

Characteristic	Agreement (percentage)	Characteristic	Agreement (percentage)
25 Hate to be told what to do	42.4	31 See things through	76.8
Like to be told what to do	19.2	Give up easily	9.1
A mix of the two	38.4	A mix of the two	14.1
26 Tolerant	59.6	32 Prefer to stand on their own	36.7
Intolerant	19.1	Prefer to merge with the crowd	40.8
A mix of the two	21.2	A mix of the two	22.4
27 Possess self-control	75.5	33 Class conscious	42.4
Lack self-control	12.3	Do not believe in class difference	30.3
A mix of the two	12.2	A mix of the two	27.3
28 Friendly	67.0	34 Able to cope with new and uncertain situations	70.0
Unfriendly	12.0	Unable to cope with new and uncertain situations	16.0
A mix of the two	21.0	A mix of the two	14.0
29 Not open to bribery	57.6	35 Prefer to be on their own	27.0
Corruptible	21.2	Prefer to be in a group	44.0
A mix of the two	21.2	A mix of the two	29.0
30 Prefer to work on their own	61.6		
Prefer to work under supervision	19.2		
A mix of the two	19.2		

Note: As mentioned in Chapter 5, pairs of opposing characteristics were placed on either end of a seven-point scale. The points were scored from 1 to 7. Points 1, 2, and 3 were taken to signify 'agreement' with one characteristic and points 5, 6, and 7 'agreement' with its opposite.

Table 7.2 Indian character

Characteristic	Agreement (percentage)	Characteristic	Agreement (percentage)
1 Interested in community affairs	74.7	7 Cope well with set-backs	72.7
Indifferent to community affairs	18.3	Do not cope well with set-backs	21.2
A mix of the two	7.1	A mix of the two	6.1
2 Honest	64.3	8 Rational	66.4
Dishonest	7.1	Irrational	21.4
A mix of the two	28.6	A mix of the two	12.2
3 Modest	55.0	9 Independent of their parents	46.5
Arrogant	23.0	Dependent on their parents	41.4
A mix of the two	22.0	A mix of the two	12.1
4 Respect the law to the letter	61.6	10 Reserved	36.0
Prepared to bend the law	22.2	Out-going	43.0
A mix of the two	16.2	A mix of the two	21.0
5 Self-confident	69.0	11 Aggressive	25.5
Lack self-confidence	16.0	Submissive	45.9
A mix of the two	15.0	A mix of the two	28.6
6 Have trust in others	56.0	12 Law abiding	72.0
Do not trust others	28.0	Law breaking	15.0
A mix of the two	16.0	A mix of the two	13.0

Table 7.2 Indian character (continued)

Characteristic	Agreement (percentage)	Characteristic	Agreement (percentage)
13 Believe in sharing fairly	39.0	19 Respect powerful people	77.0
Selfish	42.0	Do not respect powerful people	11.0
A mix of the two	19.0	A mix of the two	12.0
14 Obedient to their seniors	80.8	20 Willing to take account of others' opinions	45.4
Disobedient to their seniors	11.1	Prefer to impose their own opinion on others	34.4
A mix of the two	8.1	A mix of the two	20.2
15 Opposed to change	36.0	21 Have a strong sense of responsibility	68.0
Accept change	44.0	Have no sense of responsibility	13.0
A mix of the two	20.0	A mix of the two	19.0
16 Trustworthy	69.1	22 Play safe	42.4
Not trustworthy	12.4	Take chances	39.4
A mix of the two	18.5	A mix of the two	18.2
17 Unemotional	19.0	23 Not afraid of powerful people	31.0
Emotional	65.0	Afraid of powerful people	54.0
A mix of the two	16.0	A mix of the two	15.0
18 Disciplined	59.6	24 Do not believe in fate	14.0
Undisciplined	22.2	Believe in fate	71.0
A mix of the two	18.2	A mix of the two	15.0

Table 7.2 Indian character (continued)

Characteristic	Agreement (percentage)	Characteristic	Agreement (percentage)
25 Hate to be told what to do	26.3	31 See things through	52.8
Like to be told what to do	54.6	Give up easily	29.1
A mix of the two	19.2	A mix of the two	19.1
26 Tolerant	69.7	32 Prefer to stand on their own	37.0
Intolerant	14.2	Prefer to merge with the crowd	50.0
A mix of the two	16.2	A mix of the two	13.0
27 Possess self-control	66.6	33 Caste conscious	59.6
Lack self-control	18.2	Do not believe in class difference	30.4
A mix of the two	15.2	A mix of the two	10.1
28 Friendly	71.0	34 Able to cope with new and uncertain situations	64.0
Unfriendly	18.0	Unable to cope with new and uncertain situations	32.0
A mix of the two	11.0	A mix of the two	4.0
29 Not open to bribery	43.3	35 Prefer to be on their own	15.1
Corruptible	35.1	Prefer to be in a group	73.8
A mix of the two	21.6	A mix of the two	11.1
30 Prefer to work on their own	43.4		
Prefer to work under supervision	40.5		
A mix of the two	16.2		

Note: As mentioned in Chapter 5, pairs of opposing characteristics were placed on either end of a seven-point scale. The points were scored from 1 to 7. Points 1, 2, and 3 were taken to signify 'agreement' with one characteristic and points 5, 6, and 7 'agreement' with its opposite.

membership rather than class as it is known in Western industrial societies. However, Mehta (1982) identifies three economic classes in India. These are (1) the middle class, which is largely the product of British power and consists of educated people with no common economic or political ideology other than their interest in the new order. This class is the dominant class, but in a predominantly agricultural country it is far less powerful and influential than what Mehta calls the 'middle castes', or the rural elite. (2) The 'middle castes' who include landed proprietors, money-lenders and merchants in rural areas, and (3) the rest who are the masses.

English and Indian cultural values and attitudes

The previous sections studied the social and cultural environments in which English and Indian people are brought up and live. The remainder of the chapter discusses the findings of the cultural surveys carried out by the author in England and India in order to examine the values and attitudes that these environments are likely to inculcate and reinforce in English and Indian peoples, and it compares the two cultures as regards the characteristics studied.

Tables 7.1 and 7.2 show the results of the cultural surveys carried out in the two countries. The Tables show that there are similarities as well as differences between the two cultures.

Discipline and self-control

English sample The English, according to the sample, are a disciplined people, with control over both themselves and their emotions. The agreement on self-control and discipline is further complemented by the views expressed by a substantial proportion of the sample who regarded the English as reserved. Raynor (1969) and Parekh (1974) also believe that the English have an ability to exercise self-control over their emotions and aggression. To the author, as a person from an emotional culture, the English at first seemed unemotional and without feelings. However, on closer acquaintance, one found that they are emotional. The difference between the English and the Iranians is that the former refrain from expressing their emotions in public, which may have something to do with their love of privacy; whereas the latter are in general less inhibited about showing their feelings and emotions in the company of others.

Indian sample According to the respondents, Indian people are disciplined and value self-restraint. However, when it comes to expressing their emotions, they see themselves as less reserved and less restrained. Parekh (1974), comparing the Indians with the English, said of the former that they are emotional and display their emotions in public, even to the extent of self-indulgence. The present author too found the Indians far more emotional than the English and even the Iranians. The Indians' public display of emotion may have something to do with their relatively low concern for privacy.

Fair play and consideration for others

English sample These traits have attracted a fair amount of agreement among the respondents as being present in the English. A large number of the respondents thought the English a friendly people who believe in sharing fairly; only a small percentage of the sample thought them selfish. The sample also believed that the English prefer to take account of others' opinions. Another manifestation of the English people's feelings for others is their high public spirit and their interest in community affairs. This point was confirmed by the majority of the sample.

Many writers and commentators (see, for instance, Law, 1948; Terry, 1979; *The Times*, 10 and 22 September 1980) have also observed a 'sense of duty toward local community', 'consideration for others' feelings' and a 'highly developed public spirit' among the English.

Indian sample According to the literature, the Indians are said to be 'clannish' and community conscious. A substantial majority of the sample agreed that their compatriots are interested in community affairs. However, the 'community' to which an Indian person feels affiliated and in whose affairs he is interested seems to be his own caste, religious group, and close circle of relatives and friends, rather than society as a whole.

The Zoroastrian community in Bombay, for example, has a hospital which, except in emergency accident cases, only admits Zoroastrian patients. Mother Teresa of Calcutta, who has lived most of her life in India, in an interview with *India Today* (31 May 1983) observed that there was among the Indians a 'painfully profound' lack of love and concern for others outside their immediate circle of relatives and friends, indifference to human misery, cruelty, lack of understanding and consideration for others' feelings, lack of sense of social service, selfishness and no sense of neighbourhood. Koestler (1966) too was struck by the lack of concern of the rich Bombayites for the pavement dwellers of their city.

These observations are, to some degree, also consistent with the responses to another pair of characteristics in the questionnaire, where 41 percent of the respondents thought the Indians selfish as opposed to 39 percent who said they believe in sharing fairly. However, the Indians are a very friendly people, and once they accept someone as a friend, or even an acquaintance, they will go out of their way to be helpful. Needless to say, the author's research fieldwork in India would not have been possible without the generous assistance of dozens of Indians who did not even know her before she visited their country.

Tolerance

English sample A large percentage of the respondents thought the English people tolerant. This may indicate the tolerance of other people's opinion and ideas, in which case it is consistent with the response to the items related to 'fair play', 'interest in community affairs', and 'taking account of others' opinions' just discussed. It can, however, also be interpreted as tolerance of other people, such as foreigners and immigrants. Judging by the race-related events now taking place up and down the country and the general attitude of people towards the non-English, such as the Irish and black communities, the English seem to be an intolerant nation.

Indian sample The sample's agreement on tolerance as a trait present among the Indians is quite high. However, this is only moderately supported by the respondents' views on a related characteristic: a much smaller proportion of the respondents thought that Indian people are willing to take account of others' opinions, and as many as 34.4 percent said the Indians prefer to impose their own opinion on others. This point confirms Kakar's (1971a) views about the authoritarian nature of Indian culture. The intolerance of others' opinions is further reflected, for instance, in the violent clashes between sectarian groups in various parts of the country.

Deference

English sample Deference and obedience to seniors are, according to the sample, held strongly by the English as a virtue. Further, English people are believed to respect powerful people. However, they do not like to be ordered about and hate to be told what to do. Also, a distinction should be made between fear of powerful people and respect for them. The former was quite clearly rejected by 64 percent of the respondents who believed that the English are not afraid of powerful people.

Indian sample Obedience to seniors and respect for powerful people comes at the top of the list of traits attributed to Indian people by the sample. 90.8 percent agreed that Indian people are obedient to their seniors, and a large percentage of the sample thought the Indians like to be told what to do. The Indians are also believed to respect powerful people.
Views expressed by other writers are in line with the findings of this part of the survey. A belief that all wisdom comes from elders, respect for and fear of authority, obedience to seniors and those in authority, authoritarian dependency, preference for authoritarian leadership (Kakar, 1971a and 1971b), use of fear as a principal motive of social conduct, and authoritarian social discipline (Barua, 1982; *The Telegraph*, 18 April 1983; *India Today*, 30 April 1983) have been mentioned as characteristics of Indians and Indian society.

Individualism, collectivism

English sample An English person is said to love liberty and privacy. This should certainly be reflected in his preference for being independent and having autonomy at work. A considerable majority of the sample thought that the English are independent of their parents and that they prefer to work on their own. However, a large number of the respondents believed that the English do not want to be on their own and prefer to be in a group and merge with the crowd. These results are consistent with the arguments put forward by such writers as Jamieson (1980) and Wiener (1981) about the decline of English individualism in the course of the past two centuries or so.

Indian sample The responses to the pairs related to these characteristics confirm the communitarianism of Indian people which was discussed earlier. A very large majority of the sample agreed that the Indians prefer to be in a group and to merge with the crowd. This clearly shows that Indians are collectivist, and the group, be it community or family, takes preference over individual members.
This is consistent with Parekh's (1974) and Segal's (1971) observations that there is a high group morality among Indian people whereby freedom of the individual is subjected to the interests of the group and there is pressure for conformity to the group. Characteristics such as 'very little regard for internal private space', 'no sense of privacy for oneself', and 'averse to spatial structuring of life', which Parekh attributes to the Indians, may also be interpreted as a reflection of a high degree of group belonging and a low degree of individualism among Indian people.

Attitudes towards social stratification

English sample The English are said to be obsessed with class differentiation (Terry, 1979). In the present study only a moderate majority of the sample agreed with this view.

Indian sample Indian society is primarily stratified on the basis of caste membership. A pair of items relating to caste was included in the questionnaire to examine the extent to which Indian people believed in caste differentiation. This pair substituted for the one in the English version relating to class. In response to this pair, the majority of the respondents agreed that their compatriots are caste conscious. In the questionnaire the respondents were also asked to write to which caste they belonged. Only four respondents said they did not believe in caste differentiation, and of these two were Muslims whose religion does not approve of the caste system.

Resourcefulness

English sample A resourceful person is able to cope well with new situations and set-backs without losing his integrity and self-confidence, and to tackle problems in a 'rational' manner. It appears that the English are regarded by the sample as a resourceful people. A large percentage of the respondents believed that the English are self-confident, able to cope with set-backs, can handle new and uncertain situations, and are rational.

The sample's views on these matters are consistent with Raynor's (1969) observations. He attributes to the English individual responsibility, resourcefulness and self-reliance, curiosity, ability to think at an abstract level, and a willingness and ability to stand on their own feet intellectually. Parekh (1974) also believes the English people in general are self-confident and able to handle difficult situations.

Indian sample A large majority of the sample thought that Indian people can cope well with set-backs, are able to handle new and uncertain situations, and are self-confident. While in India, the author was told of many cases where people had lost their jobs, homes, land and relatives in natural disasters, such as flood and drought, but with the support of relatives and friends they had worked hard and started anew. This point is clearly reflected in the favourable responses given to two pairs of questions relating to ability to cope with adversity. It further suggests the tenacity of Indian people which is also reflected in the sample's response to another item in the questionnaire, where a moderate majority of the respondents agreed that the Indians see things through.

Honesty and trust

English sample The majority of respondents thought the English trustworthy and honest, not open to bribery, and to have trust in others. Honesty and trust have been suggested also by Rowntree and Lavers (1951), Almond and Verba (1963) and many other writers as salient characteristics present in the English. However, Parekh (1974), an Indian writer, believes that they are distrustful and suspicious of others. Having come from a different culture, Iran, where the state of trust among people in general is very low, and the public administration is bedevilled by corruption, the author regards the English as more honest and trusting than the Iranians.

Indian sample The majority of the respondents believed that Indians are honest and trustworthy and have trust in others. However, the percentage drops considerably when the Indians are rated on corruption. Only 43.3 percent agreed that the Indians are not open to bribery and 35.1 percent thought they are corrupt. The explanation perhaps is that acceptance of bribes, which usually takes place within the government bureaucracies, is not considered an act of dishonesty, since it does not take place at a personal level; that is, with one's relatives and friends. Rather, it is done against an impersonal body which is an 'outsider'.

Other observers of Indian society have also noticed people's distrust and suspicion towards politicians and those in authority (Segal, 1971), low morality and considerable corruption in public service, tax evasion, embezzlement, and fabrication of accounts (*Indian Express*, 1 and 29 March 1983; *India Today*, 31 March 1983).

Attitudes toward the law

English sample A great majority of the respondents agreed that the English are law-abiding and respect the law to the letter. The English people's attitudes to law may be a reflection of their love of privacy. Law can be viewed as a means to protect people against intrusion by outsiders in their affairs. It can also reflect orderliness and discipline which, as was discussed earlier, are among the characteristics attributed to the English.

Respect for law and order, appreciation of the police, decency and, paradoxically, 'fiddling', have been said by many writers to be present in the English (e.g. Gorer, 1955; Terry, 1979). Fiddling, however, is directed against authorities, that is, non-persons rather than against individuals.

An example of the English people's respect for law which struck the author in her early days in England was their driving habits and careful observation of traffic rules, such as maintaining sufficient distance from the car in front, using indicators, stopping for red lights in the middle of the night when there was no other car in sight, stopping at pedestrian crossings, and so on. None of these rules are observed to such an extent in Iran. I later travelled in France, India and Belgium and found drivers there behaved more like Iranian drivers than the English.

Indian sample The Indians are considered by the sample as a law-abiding people. As a matter of fact, both in England and India, I had many encounters with various Indian officials in my efforts to obtain permission to carry out this research, and to extend my leave to stay in the country for a few weeks beyond the initial visa period. The insistence of the Indian officials on doing everything according to the laws, rules and regulations prescribed in every minute detail was a good example of the rules and laws being followed to the letter by the people in charge of affairs. However, many officials are prepared to bend, or even ignore, the rules and directives for their friends and relatives, and, in some cases, for money. I had to appeal to them to get things done a little faster mainly through my friends and connections.

Acceptance of responsibility, dependence on others

English sample A very large majority of respondents thought that English people have a strong sense of responsibility. This view is consistent with some other characteristics, such as resourcefulness, self-confidence, independence, and honesty, which were discussed earlier and which are attributed by observers to the English in general.

Indian sample The sample believed that Indian people have a strong sense of responsibility. However, the high score on responsibility is not matched with high scores on items related to independence. As was discussed earlier, the Indians appear to be dependent on their parents and prefer to work under supervision. This may be a reflection of the Indian people's collectivism, where people are emotionally and financially dependent on each other, rather than the inability to accept responsibility as an individual. Conservatism and fatalism are also among the characteristics attributed to the English and Indians respectively.

English conservatism
The English are known to be a nation with a love for the past and for traditions. Only some of those questioned, however, agreed with this view. 42 percent of the respondents thought that the English people are opposed to change and 37.4 percent thought they play safe. Nevertheless, the love of the past, traditionalism, reluctance to change and conservatism are clearly manifest in the careful preservation of old buildings and monuments, and in the observation of detail in public ceremonies, such as the annual pageantry surrounding the opening of Parliament which has its roots in centuries-old traditions.

Indian fatalism
The majority of the respondents said that Indian people believe in fate and are submissive. Segal (1971) argues that fatalism, acceptance of status quo, submissiveness, resignation and acceptance of social differentiation and any form of human suffering are perceived by the Indians as a means of cleansing themselves of their past. However, the present author's observations and experience in India contradict these assertions. The militancy of trade unions, the months-old strike by workers in textile factories in Bombay and in power stations in Calcutta for better wages and other working conditions can hardly be 'acceptance of status quo' and 'acceptance of any form of human suffering'. The author once witnessed a very long procession of domestic servants marching through the streets of Bombay demanding the right to belong to trade unions, to have fixed working hours, and to have paid annual leave.

DISCUSSION

The findings of the present surveys and the literature on English and Indian societies show that there is a high degree of consistency between, on the one hand, the attitudes and values held by English and Indian peoples in general and, on the other, their upbringing at home and later socialization processes in society. For instance, English people place a great emphasis on their children's independence and autonomy. This emphasis is fostered by the 'Protestant ethic' and reinforced at school and other educational institutions through the teaching methods which are largely based on self-discovery and experimentation. One would expect that a person who is brought up in an environment such as this would be highly independent, individualistic and able to stand on her own feet. The results of the survey

Cultural and organizational assessment

Table 7.3 *Comparison of English and Indian cultural characteristics as reported by respondents to the culture questionnaire*

	English ($N = 100$)	Indian ($N = 100$)	Value of 't'	Level of confidence (p)
Independent of their parents	2.72	3.92	4.60	0.000
Not afraid of powerful people	3.01	4.40	5.74	0.000
Do not believe in fate	3.94	5.25	5.55	0.000
Hate to be told what to do	3.41	4.47	4.64	0.000
Prefer to work on their own	2.83	3.80	3.82	0.000
See things through	2.36	3.49	5.35	0.000
Prefer to be on their own	4.27	5.14	3.70	0.000
Unemotional	4.01	4.95	4.32	0.000
Respect powerful people	3.82	2.54	−5.78	0.000
Aggressive	3.56	4.29	3.45	0.001
Not open to bribery	2.96	3.80	3.51	0.001
Believe in sharing fairly	3.31	4.10	3.44	0.001
Have a strong sense of responsibility	2.25	2.83	2.88	0.004
Cope well with set-backs	2.45	3.02	2.69	0.008
Obedient to their seniors	3.08	2.54	−2.45	0.015
Honest	2.43	2.88	2.40	0.017
Trustworthy	2.34	2.81	2.38	0.018
Disciplined	2.76	3.26	2.29	0.023
Modest	3.77	3.26	−2.28	0.024
Reserved	3.80	4.35	2.21	0.028
Able to cope with new and uncertain situations	2.88	3.34	1.85	0.065
Willing to take account of others' opinions	3.77	3.82	0.24	0.810
Possess self-control	2.66	3.00	1.62	0.106
Interested in community affairs	3.24	2.89	−1.56	0.122
Law-abiding	2.60	2.92	1.47	0.144
Class/caste conscious	3.84	3.48	−1.41	0.161
Self-confident	2.71	2.96	1.15	0.253
Respect the law to the letter	3.38	3.14	−1.04	0.302
Have trust in others	3.14	3.37	0.96	0.340
Prefer to stand on their own	4.01	4.24	0.88	0.381
Tolerant	3.00	2.82	−0.79	0.432
Friendly	2.68	2.83	0.69	0.490
Rational	3.10	3.15	0.21	0.832
Opposed to change	4.17	4.21	0.16	0.876
Play safe	3.83	3.81	−0.08	0.937

Note: The lower the score, the more the characteristic is present in the culture. The higher the score, the more the opposite is present.

conducted in England confirm this: the English see themselves as independent, resourceful, self-confident and able to cope with setbacks. The same degree of consistency exists in the case of the Indian survey. For instance, dependence on parents, open expression of emotions, preference to belong to a group, respect for and obedience to seniors, fear of the powerful, and belief in fate, are all consistent with family structure, child-rearing practices, Hindu religious doctrines, and learning experiences at school and in the society as a whole.

Table 7.3 summarizes the findings of the surveys and shows that the two samples differ significantly from one another on twenty characteristics: The Indians compared to the English are more obedient to their seniors, are more afraid of and respect powerful people, and hate less to be told what to do. These appear to be consistent with Indian and English people's respective upbringing, family structure and educational experiences.

The Indians are also more dependent on their parents, more emotional, less disciplined, less tenacious, and less able to cope with set-backs and new and uncertain situations. These, again, are consistent with child-rearing practices and teaching methods at schools in the two countries.

The English prefer to be, and work, on their own and are more reserved than the Indians. This is consistent with the English people's love of privacy and an emphasis on individuality and independence, and the Indian people's preference for conformity, extended family, and dependent emotional relationships between its members.

The English believe less in fate compared to the Indians. This appears to be consistent with their respective religious beliefs and doctrines.

The English are more honest and trustworthy and less open to bribery compared with the Indians. This is consistent with a relatively low level of corruption in the public administration in England and a much higher and more pervasive level of corruption in Indian government bureaucracies.

The Indians believe less in sharing fairly than do the English, which is consistent with the former's communitarianism and the latter's belief in 'fair play'.

ENGLISH AND INDIAN WORK-RELATED ATTITUDES – HYPOTHESES

Chapter 5 defined organizational structure as a framework for decision making and decision implementation. The decision process as a whole was argued to involve power and authority relationships;

Table 7.4 *Hypotheses about the influence of English and Indian cultures on work-related attitudes and their consequences for work organizations in England and India*

Cultural aspects	Rationale	Hypotheses — Work-related attitudes	Hypotheses — Consequences for organization
Power and authority relationships	Indian people are more obedient to their seniors, respect powerful people more, and are less adverse to being told what to do compared with English people	H. 1: Indian employees will perceive a larger power distance between themselves and their managers (lower perception of power) compared with English employees	H. 2: Indian organizations will be more centralized than their English counterparts
Ambiguity and uncertainty	English people are more able to cope with new and uncertain situations compared with Indian people	H. 3: The degree of tolerance of ambiguity will be higher (lower uncertainty avoidance) among English employees compared with Indian employees	H. 4: Indian organizations will be more specialized and formalized (more use of laid-down rules) compared with the English companies
Commitment: (a) Motivation	Indian people are more fatalist than the English	H. 5: Indian employees will have lower expectations from their organization and are therefore more easily motivated. This will be reflected in their higher satisfaction with their company compared with the English employees	
(b) Individualism	Indian people have a lower preference to work on their own (higher preference to work in a group) and a lower preference for being on their own (higher preference to merge with the crowd) compared with the English	H. 6: Indian employees will be less individualistic than English employees	

Category		
Trust	H. 7: Indian employees will score higher on the two components of commitment and they are therefore expected to express a higher degree of commitment to their organization compared to the English employees	H. 8: Indian managers will employ a more relaxed control system compared to the English managers
	H. 9: On the whole the state of trust will be the same among Indian and English employees	H. 10: Managers in both countries will employ similar control systems
Expectations from a job	H. 11: Autonomy at work and freedom to do one's work will be of greater importance to English employees than they will be to the Indian employees	H. 12: Authority and decision-making power are delegated lower down the hierarchy in English organizations compared with their Indian counterparts
	H. 13: Good pay and other financial benefits will be of less importance to Indian employees than to English employees	H. 14: Reward and punishment policies will be more financially-oriented in English firms than in Indian firms
Management philosophy	H. 15: English employees will have a more egalitarian view regarding management practices and favour more a participative style compared with Indian employees	H. 16: There will be more consultation and communication in English organizations compared with their Indian counterparts

The English are more honest and trustworthy, and are less open to bribery compared with Indian people. However, both peoples appear to be law-abiding and law-respecting, and have trust in others

The English value individuality and self-determination more than the Indians

Indian people are said to be less materialistic in outlook than the English, despite their massive poverty

Both people believe in a social hierarchy. However, the class system in England is less rigid and inequalities are less marked than is the case in Indian society ambiguity, uncertainty and risk taking; reliability, honesty and trust; dedication, loyalty and commitment; motivation, control and discipline, and communication. The chapter then hypothesized about the likely influence of culture on these aspects of organization.

With respect to the above definition of organizational structure and the relationships, processes and actions which may surround it, a series of specific hypotheses are here advanced about the likely impact of English and Indian cultures on organizational members' work-related attitudes and about the implications of these for organizational structure. Table 7.4 shows these hypotheses.

Chapters 8 and 9 will discuss the findings of the surveys carried out in a sample of manufacturing firms in England and India to put these hypotheses to test.

8
Cultures, Work-Related Attitudes, and Organizational Structure

The previous chapter compared the present-day cultural and socioeconomic characteristics of England and India. The chapter advanced some hypotheses, following a culturalist framework, about the state of Indian and English employees' work-related attitudes and their likely consequences for their organizations. The present chapter discusses the findings of the surveys carried out in the two countries to test these hypotheses. It is assumed that to the extent that the hypotheses are supported by the findings, the arguments of the writers following a culturalist perspective may offer a valid model for understanding Indian and English organizations. To the extent that the hypotheses are rejected, the culturalist perspective's model is inadequate, and there is a need to look for non-cultural explanations.

THE SAMPLES

Employees

The English sample consisted of 343 employees. These were all born and brought up in England and their families' origins were English for at least three generations. The Indian sample consisted of 337 employees who lived in Bombay and nearby cities and were all of Indian origin for at least three generations. A vast majority of the respondents came from the southern states of Maharashtra, Karala and Karnataka. The regional backgrounds of this sample were very similar to that of the survey which was carried out at an earlier stage of the study (Chapter 7) to examine the cultural characteristics of Indian people. Any differences between the degree of values and attitudes held by the two samples are therefore likely to be for reasons other than regional cultural differences.

The occupational positions of the two samples covered a wide range, falling into the following broad categories: directors and other senior managers, supervisors, engineers and technicians, specialists, office workers and shopfloor manual employees. The level of education among Indian respondents was much higher than that of the English sample. The average age of the former was 34 and that of the latter 37 years. Over 75 percent of English respondents were Protes-

108 *Cultural and organizational assessment*

tant and 73 percent of the Indian sample were Hindus. For the Indian employees a further question concerning their caste was also included in the questionnaire, but very few people chose to answer it. It must be pointed out that statistical tests showed no significant differences between different religious categories within each country on the work attitudes which were studied.

Finally, given the diversity of Indian culture, it is not assumed that the Indian employees who participated in the study are representative of Indian employees in general. However, for convenience and simplicity, the sample will be referred to as Indian employees.

Organizations

Seven organizations in each country were selected and matched in pairs across the two countries for their major contextual variables in terms of stability and complexity. These organizations were manufacturing firms engaged in a varied range of industries. Their size, in terms of the number of employees, ranged from 133 to 1,670 (see also Chapter 6). In order to maintain anonymity of the organizations, each one is given a pseudonym which corresponds to the industry in which it is engaged and to its country of origin, and by which it will

Table 8.1 *Contextual characteristics of the fourteen organizations*

Contextual factors	Pair One		Pair Two	
	Brew E	Brew I	Sweet E	Soft I
Industry	Brewery	Brewery	Confectionery	Soft drinks
Product	Beer	Beer	Sweets	Soft drinks
Technology	Simple, stable	Simple, stable	Simple, stable	Simple, stable
Size	213	258	143	133
Status	Independent with production units	Independent	Independent with production units	Independent with production units
Ownership	Family	Family	Family	Family
Control	Salaried managers + owner executive chairman and president	Salaried managers + owner executive directors	Members of the family	Members of the family and salaried managers
Age (years)	134	15	55	34
Market share (%)	9.1	40–45	20	60

Table 8.1 (continued)

	Pair Three		Pair Four	
Contextual factors	Chem E	Chem I	Pharm E	Pharm I
Industry	Chemicals	Chemicals	Pharmaceuticals	Pharmaceuticals
Product	Chemical compounds and dyestuff	Chemical compounds	Wide range of drugs and medical products	Wide range of drugs and medical products
Technology	Simple, infrequent changes	Simple, infrequent changes	Simple, standard formulation, minor changes	Simple, standard formulation, minor changes
Size	1470	1670	268	284
Status	Autonomous subsidiary	Independent	Independent	Independent
Ownership	Parent group	Public shareholders	Family	Family
Control	Salaried managers	Salaried managers	Members of the family	Salaried managers and owner chairman
Age (years)	16	16	144	48
Market share (%)	15	20–30	1	1

be referred to in the chapter. For example, Chem I is the Indian organization which produces chemicals, and Chem E is its English counterpart. Table 8.1 shows the contextual characteristics of the organizations in the two countries, each in comparison with its counterparts.

RESULTS

1. Attitude to power and organization (Hypotheses 1 and 2)

Employees' attitude to power and authority

Hypothesis 1: Indian employees will perceive a larger power distance between themselves and their bosses (lower perception of power) compared to the English employees.

There were seventeen questions in the attitudes survey questionnaire which were related to this hypothesis, of which seven items had been

Table 8.1 (continued)

Contextual factors	Pair Five		Pair Six	
	Hi-tech E	Hi-tech I	Electron E	Electron I
Industry	Electronics	Electronics	Electronics	Electronics
Product	Electrical and electronic precision measuring instruments	Electronic equipment and components	Electronic power supplies	Electronic components for industry
Technology	Complex, not rapid change, rapid design change, several new products a year	Complex, not rapid change, rapid design change, several new products a year	Complex, standard electronic technology, rapid change in electronic components, continuous change in product design	Complex, continuous change in production process, continuous change in product design
Size	550	450	220	320
Status	Autonomous subsidiary	Independent	Autonomous subsidiary	Independent
Ownership	Parent group	Private shareholders	Parent group	Private shareholders
Control	Salaried managers	Salaried managers	Salaried managers	Salaried managers and owner chairman
Age (years)	60	37	21	20
Market share (%)	10	30	10	50 for some, 80–90 for others

Table 8.1 (continued)

Contextual factors	Pair Seven	
	Computer E	Silicon I
Industry	Electronics	Electronics
Product	High technology computer systems	Semiconductors, silicon rectifier equipment
Technology	Complex, continuous change in production process, continuous change in product design	Complex, continuous change in production process, continuous change in product design
Size	650	620
Status	Autonomous subsidiary	Independent
Ownership	Parent group	Public shareholders
Control	Salaried managers	Salaried managers
Age (years)	14	25
Market share (%)	Over 50	40–50

Note: Reproduced from *Organization Studies* 8/3, 1987.

Cultures and organizational structure 111

taken from Hofstede's power distance measure. The remainder were designed to complement these and will be discussed under the heading 'perceived power'.

Power distance Responses to power distance items are shown in Tables 8.2 to 8.4. The codes for some items in the Tables were reversed in order to maintain consistency between the scores and the direction that they indicated. These items do not form a composite

Table 8.2 *Power distance*

Items	English (mean)	Indian (mean)	Value of 't'	Level of confidence (p)
1 How often, in your experience, are employees afraid to disagree with their boss?	2.97	3.10	−1.57	0.117
2 If an employee took a complaint to a higher position than his/her immediate boss, do you think he/she would suffer later on for doing this?	2.00	2.26	−3.69	0.000
3 How often is your immediate boss concerned to help you getting ahead?	2.85	2.15	8.04	0.000
4 Employees lose respect for the boss who asks them for their advice before he makes a decision	2.39	2.42	−0.36	0.718
5 Employees should participate more in decisions made by their boss	3.58	3.60	−0.28	0.779

Note: The higher the score, the smaller the power distance.

Table 8.3 *Perceived boss*

	English (percentage)	Indian (percentage)
1 Boss 1 (tells)	23.3	18.6
2 Boss 2 (sells)	28.9	27.4
3 Boss 3 (consults)	27.4	28.7
4 Boss 4 (joins)	7.7	17.7
5 None of the above	12.7	7.6
Mean score	3.42	3.31
Value of 't' = 1.13		
Level of confidence = 0.260		

Note: Perceived bosses 1 + 2 = high power distance.

Table 8.4 *Preferred boss*

	English (percentage)	Indian (percentage)
1 Boss 1 (tells)	8.5	8.4
2 Boss 2 (sells)	29.6	26.6
3 Boss 3 (consults)	42.2	42.2
4 Boss 4 (joins)	19.6	22.8
Mean score	2.27	2.20
Value of 't' = 0.93		
Level of confidence = 0.351		

Note: Preference for bosses 1 + 2 = high power distance.

measure and the scores therefore cannot be aggregated. The pattern of responses to some items point to a larger power distance perceived by English employees, and to others by the Indian employees. The difference between the two samples is significant for two items only: Indian employees thought to a lesser degree that if they took a complaint over their boss's head they would suffer later, and they perceived their immediate boss as less concerned to help them get ahead, compared to the English sample.

Perceived power This section consisted of ten questions each of which underlined a concept related to power. These questions do not form a composite measure and the scores therefore cannot be aggregated. Table 8.5 shows the results. The two samples were different from one another on nine items. The direction of the differences in all except one indicates that English employees perceived themselves and their colleagues to enjoy greater power than did the Indian employees: English employees were less afraid to disagree with their boss, they called each other by the first name, they had easier access to their boss, they were less obedient and loyal to their superior, they considered obedience and respect for authority less of a virtue, they agreed less that a good employee does not contradict the boss, they believed less that people in authority are more knowledgeable and intelligent than their subordinates, they were more prepared to argue with people in higher positions, but they perceived themselves to have less chance of a say in the decisions which concerned their job, compared to their Indian counterparts.

The results of this section of the survey is consistent with English and Indian cultural characteristics, as discussed in Chapter 7, and also with Hypothesis 1, which speculated a higher perception of power by the English employees.

Table 8.5 *Perceived power*

Items	English (mean)	Indian (mean)	Value of 't'	Level of confidence (p)
1 People here are not afraid to disagree with their boss if they think he/she is wrong in a particular case	3.55	3.14	4.66	0.000
2 Here we call each other by first name	4.54	2.74	21.69	0.000
3 It is very easy for most of us to have access to our boss	4.21	3.82	4.46	0.000
4 Most of us here are obedient and loyal to our superiors	2.39	2.13	3.31	0.001
5 Everybody here has an equal chance to have a say in the decisions which concern our job	2.78	3.15	−4.00	0.000
6 A good employee here is the one who does not contradict his/her boss on 'important' issues	3.27	2.85	3.99	0.000
7 Obedience and respect for authority are the most important virtues children should learn	2.16	1.74	5.51	0.000
8 People in authority are usually more intelligent and more knowledgeable than their subordinates	3.38	2.86	5.63	0.000
9 Employees should receive equal salaries regardless of the position they hold in the hierarchy	2.00	2.07	−0.72	0.474
10 I am prepared to argue openly with people in higher positions	3.66	3.30	4.37	0.001
Alpha coefficient	0.15	0.23		
K-R8 coefficient	0.41	0.45		

Note: For each of items 1 to 6 there was a five-point answer scale ranging from 'definitely true' to 'definitely false', for others the answer scales ranged from 'strongly agree' to 'strongly disagree'. The responses were coded in such a manner that a higher score indicates a higher degree of perceived power.

Consequences of employees' perception of power for organizational structure

Hypothesis 2: Indian organizations will be more centralized than their English counterparts.

Table 8.6 shows the scores for centralization, delegation, joint deci-

Table 8.6 Structural dimensions of English and Indian organizations

Dimensions	English			Indian			p
	mean	sd	range	mean	sd	range	
Centralization	210	15.29	190–227	214	20.76	175–236	0.48
Delegation	167	24.44	140–227	153	20.41	132–181	0.08
Joint Decisions	19	14.27	3–45	17	9.80	4–35	0.84
Communication with:							
– boss	2.40	0.17	2.1–3.4	2.23	0.22	2.0–2.6	0.09
– subordinates	3.00	0.19	2.6–3.2	2.49	0.38	2.0–3.0	0.01
– colleagues	3.36	0.20	3.0–3.7	2.32	0.23	1.8–2.5	0.001
– people from other areas of work	2.34	0.37	1.8–2.7	2.02	0.18	1.7–2.2	0.09
– people from outside the company	1.96	0.35	1.4–2.4	2.24	0.18	1.9–2.5	0.09
Specialization	10	4.91	3–15	8.71	5.34	3–16	0.65
Formalization	12	2.57	9–17	4.71	1.11	3–6	0.001
Job-description sub-scale	3.23	0.48	3–4	1.00	1.29	0–3	0.001
Chief Executive's span of control	7	1.15	5–8	9	5.18	4–20	0.001
Number of hierarchical levels (height)	6	0.31	5–7	5.57	1.51	4–8	0.43

Notes: 'p' is the Mann–Whitney two-tailed p. Reproduced from *Organization Studies* 8/3, 1987.

sions (and other structural dimensions) for the fourteen organizations. The two samples scored similarly on centralization and joint decisions measures, but on the delegation scale the English sample scored higher (mean = 167) than did the Indian sample (mean = 153). The difference between the two samples on this scale is not significant (p = 0.08) but is high enough to be worthy of note. Hypothesis 2 appears to be rejected. However, it is also possible that the items, borrowed from the Aston Programme and employed to measure centralization and its related scales, were not able to reflect the cultural characteristics of the employees, especially their attitudes to power. Moreover, these scales were computed on the basis of the information given by the senior managers in the participating organizations. In order to examine the perception of ordinary employees of the degree of centralization, five items were included in the attitudes survey questionnaire. The responses to these items are given in Table 8.7.

Table 8.7 Perceived autonomy

Items	English (mean)	Indian (mean)	Value of 't'	Level of confidence (p)
1 People here are allowed to do as they please	2.36	2.33	0.34	0.733
2 I feel I am my own boss in most matters	3.26	2.79	4.80	0.000
3 Going through the proper channel is constantly stressed here	2.54	2.70	−1.63	0.104
4 A person can make his/her decisions without checking with anybody else	2.64	2.32	3.82	0.000
5 Whatever problem we have, we are expected to go to the same person for an answer	3.25	2.71	5.33	0.000

Note: For each item there was a five-point answer scale ranging from 'definitely true' to 'definitely false', and the responses were coded in such a manner that a higher score indicates a higher degree of perceived autonomy.

As the Table shows, English employees perceived themselves to have more autonomy at work than did the Indian employees. The two samples were significantly different from one another on three items: English employees perceived themselves more to be their own boss in most matters, they could make decisions without checking with anybody else, and they were less expected to go to the same person for an answer to their various problems. The direction of the difference between the two samples is consistent with their respective cultural backgrounds, and supports Hypothesis 2. The items used in this section reflect the respondents' cultural characteristics better than the ones borrowed from the Aston Programme.

The results of this section of the survey confirms Maurice's (1976: 5–6) criticism of the methods employed by proponents of the 'culture-free' thesis to verify their arguments:

> ... Thus, when certain formal characteristics of organization structures (centralization, formalization, specialization, etc) are related to such contextual variables as size and technology, it is important to realize that these studies are based on concepts and indicators that by nature are universal – thereby precluding any testing of the impact of national or cultural variables in which such studies express interest.

116 *Cultural and organizational assessment*

2. Tolerance of ambiguity and organization (Hypotheses 3 and 4)

Employees' tolerance of ambiguity and uncertainty

Hypothesis 3: The degree of tolerance of ambiguity will be higher (lower uncertainty avoidance) among English employees compared to Indian employees.

There were twenty-one questions related to this hypothesis in the attitudes survey questionnaire. Of these, ten were Hofstede's items for uncertainty avoidance measure. The remaining items were included to complement them and will be discussed under the heading 'tolerance of ambiguity'.

Uncertainty avoidance Table 8.8 illustrates the responses to the uncertainty avoidance items. The codes for some items had to be reversed in order to maintain consistency between the responses and the directions they indicated. The items did not cluster tightly together and the scores for them are not therefore aggregated. The two samples were significantly different from one another on four items, but the mixed directions of the differences on these and other items point to an overall lack of discrimination between the two samples: English employees agreed more that company rules should be broken when the employee thinks it is in the company's best interests. They also thought they would continue to work for their company for a shorter period than did their Indian counterparts. Indian respondents were more satisfied with their organization and had higher preference to work for a foreign boss than did their English counterparts.

Tolerance of ambiguity This section consists of eleven questions, five of which had been adopted from Child and Partridge's (1982) 'personal flexibility' scale. The questions shared a common underlying reference to change and uncertainty. Table 8.9 shows the responses to these items. The eleven items in this section had high enough alpha and K-R8 reliability coefficients (see the Table) for both samples to be regarded collectively as a composite scale. A tolerance for ambiguity index for each country was therefore calculated by aggregating the individual scores for the above eleven items. The possible range for the index is from 11 to 55. English sample scored 36 and the Indian sample 34 on the index (figures are rounded). A '*t*' test indicated a statistically significant difference between the two samples ($p < 0.001$). The direction of this difference is consistent with the samples' respective cultural background. Hypothesis 3 is not rejected.

Cultures and organizational structure 117

Table 8.8 *Uncertainty avoidance*

Items	English (mean)	Indian (mean)	Value of 't'	Level of confidence (p)
1 Company rules should not be broken even when the employee thinks it is in the company's best interest	2.97	3.29	−3.44	0.001
2 How long do you think you will continue to work for this organization?	2.85	3.01	−2.02	0.037
3 How often do you feel nervous or tense at work?	2.20	2.25	−0.73	0.466
4 If you had a choice of promotion to either a managerial or specialist position, and these were at the same salary level, which would appeal to you most?	2.96	3.10	−1.28	0.200
5 Considering everything, how would you rate your overall satisfaction with this organization at the present time?	4.56	4.97	−4.31	0.000
6 How do you feel about working for a boss who is from a country other than your own?	2.22	1.94	6.88	0.000
7 Decisions made by individuals are usually of a higher quality than decisions made by groups	3.35	3.34	0.06	0.95
8 Most organizations will be better off if conflict can be eliminated	3.97	3.92	0.74	0.457
9 Employees lose respect for the boss who asks them for their advice before he makes a decision*	3.60	3.57	0.36	0.718
10 Competition between employees usually does more harm than good	3.04	3.07	−0.29	0.77
Alpha coefficient**	−0.26	−0.01		

Notes: The higher the score, the higher the avoidance of uncertainty.

* This item was also included in the power distance section, but the codes have been reversed here (see Hofstede, 1980 for details).
** K-R8 coefficient cannot be computed for the uncertainty avoidance items because the answer scales for the items are not similar.

Table 8.9 Tolerance for ambiguity

Items	English (mean)	Indian (mean)	Value of 't'	Level of confidence (p)
1 I would generally prefer to do something I am used to rather than something that is different*	3.20	3.19	0.10	0.919
2 It is more fun to tackle a complicated problem than to solve a simple one	3.99	4.07	−1.09	0.277
3 I enjoy finding myself in new and unusual circumstances*	3.67	3.63	0.53	0.594
4 People who fit their lives to schedule probably miss most of the joy of living	3.50	3.38	1.38	0.167
5 I am in favour of a very strict enforcement of all laws no matter what the consequence	3.23	2.88	3.94	0.000
6 A good job is one where what is to be done and how it is done are always clear	2.62	2.08	6.39	0.000
7 I do not like to undertake any project unless I have a pretty good idea as to how it will turn out	3.00	2.43	7.04	0.000
8 I get a lot of pleasure from taking on new problems*	3.85	3.99	−2.07	0.039
9 I would prefer a job which is always changing*	3.46	2.97	5.43	0.000
10 People who seem unsure and uncertain about things make me feel uncomfortable	2.60	2.20	5.20	0.000
11 I like to have a regular pattern in my working day*	3.16	2.88	3.08	0.002
Tolerance for ambiguity score	36	34	6.41	0.000
Personal flexibility score	17	17	0.00	1.000
Alpha coefficient	0.69	0.52		
K-R8 coefficient	0.76	0.63		

Notes: For each item there was a five-point answer scale ranging from 'strongly agree' to 'strongly disagree', and the responses were coded in such a manner that a higher score indicates a higher degree of tolerance for ambiguity.

* These items are adopted from Child and Partridge (1982).

Cultures and organizational structure 119

Consequences of employees' tolerance of ambiguity for organizational structure

Hypothesis 4: Indian organizations will be more formalized (use laid-down rules and regulations to a greater extent) and more specialized compared to their English counterparts.

Formalization As Table 8.6 shows, Indian organizations were far less formalized (average score of 5) than were the English companies (average score of 12). The Mann–Whitney test showed a significant difference between the two samples ($p = 0.001$). It has been argued that an organization's degree of formalization is influenced by its age – older organizations use more written rules and documentation (Inkson et al., 1970). The average age for the present samples is 28 and 68 years respectively, but when age was controlled for, the Indian firms still scored much lower than the English firms.

Hypothesis 4, as far as formalization is concerned, is rejected. However, this rejection concerns the speculated relationship between the employees' tolerance of ambiguity, as a cultural trait, and the degree of formalization of their work organization.

A closer examination of English and Indian organizations' scores on formalization, and of some aspects of their cultures, leads to some interesting observations. Four of the items which comprised the formalization scale were concerned with job descriptions. Job descriptions can be argued to reflect, among other things, people's preferences for clear-cut territorial boundaries around their jobs and the spatial and social distance they may wish to maintain between themselves and others. As Table 8.6 shows, Indian organizations scored considerably lower on the job-description sub-scale than did their English counterparts, which means that they had fewer written job descriptions. This difference of scores is quite consistent with the two organizations' respective cultures. As was discussed in Chapter 7, Indian and English peoples have been depicted as being diametrically opposed with regard to such concepts as spatiality, privacy, and independence. Indian culture is characterized by a lack of concern with privacy, and by close physical and emotional proximity and dependence; whereas English culture is characterized by the love of privacy, independence, and the maintenance of a certain physical and emotional space (see also Parekh, 1974; Terry, 1979).

Specialization As Table 8.6 shows there is no difference between English and Indian organizations' scores on the specialization dimension. The connection between specialization and employees' tolerance of ambiguity and uncertainty as speculated in Hypothesis 4 is rejected.

3. Commitment and organization
   (Hypotheses 5, 6, 7, 8)

Employees' commitment

Chapter 5 argued that employees will commit themselves to their work organizations if, among other things, they are motivated and have a high sense of group-orientation (low individualism). There were sixteen items in the attitudes survey questionnaire which were used to measure these concepts.

Motivation

Hypothesis 5: Indian employees will have lower expectations from their work organizations and are therefore more easily motivated than the English employees. This will be reflected in a higher satisfaction with the organization among the Indian employees.

There was one item in the uncertainty avoidance section which concerned the respondents' satisfaction with their organization. English employees scored 4.56 and the Indian employees 4.97 on this item. The difference between the two groups was significant ($p<0.001$). Hypothesis 5 is not rejected.

Individualism

Hypothesis 6: Indian employees will be less individualistic than the English employees.

This section consisted of six items which were designed to measure the respondents' degree of individualism. These items do not form a composite measure because their internal reliability coefficients were poor. Table 8.10 illustrate the responses to the items. As the Table shows, the two samples are significantly different from one another on three items: (a) it was more important to English employees that their job left them sufficient time for their personal life than it was to the Indian employees. (b) The latter would like more to stand on their own, and (c) they believed more that they could learn better by 'striking out' alone than did their English counterparts.

The relatively high scores of the Indian employees indicate the rejection of hypothesis 6, which was based on the literature and on the findings of the cultural surveys carried out by the author in the two countries.

Table 8.10 *Individualism*

Items	English (mean)	Indian (mean)	Value of '*t*'	Level of confidence (*p*)
1 I prefer to make up my own mind on things only after seeking advice from friends	3.02	3.10	−0.84	0.404
2 It is important to me that my job leaves me sufficient time for my personal life	4.23	3.45	9.45	0.000
3 I would like to stand on my own in life rather than relying on others	3.96	4.39	−6.08	0.000
4 I prefer to merge with the crowd than stand on my own	3.46	3.30	1.85	0.065
5 I feel uncomfortable going against the view of a majority	3.37	3.22	1.74	0.083
6 One can learn better by striking out alone than one can by following the advice of others	2.89	3.45	−6.33	0.000
Alpha coefficient	0.18	0.21		
K-R8 coefficient	0.51	0.51		

Note: For each item there was a five-point answer scale ranging from 'strongly agree' to 'strongly disagree', and the responses were coded in such a manner that a higher score indicates a higher degree of individualism.

Employees' level of commitment

Hypothesis 7: Indian employees are expected to express a higher degree of commitment to their work organizations than are the English employees.

There were nine items in the questionnaire which were related to the concept of commitment and had been adopted from Cook and Wall (1980). Responses to these items are shown in Table 8.11. The consistency among the items in this section was very high for both samples and the internal reliability tests showed that they could be treated collectively as a composite measure (see the Table). A commitment index for each sample was computed by aggregating the individual scores for the nine items. The possible range was from 9 to 45. English employees scored 34 on this index and the Indian employees 35 (figures are rounded). The difference between the two groups is not significant ($p = 0.19$). Hypothesis 7 is rejected.

Table 8.11 Commitment

Items	English (mean)	Indian (mean)	Value of 't'	Level of confidence (p)
1 I would be pleased to know that my own work has made a contribution to the good of the company	4.46	4.45	0.22	0.826
2 Sometimes I feel like leaving this organization	3.27	3.30	−0.32	0.752
3 I would not recommend a close friend to join this organization	3.67	3.34	2.95	0.003
4 I am not willing to put myself out just to help this organization	4.13	3.86	2.79	0.005
5 I am quite proud to be able to tell people which organization I work for	3.79	4.18	−4.34	0.000
6 Even if I had a choice of another job, I would be reluctant to leave this organization	3.12	3.11	0.09	0.929
7 I feel myself to be part of this organization	3.85	4.42	−7.55	0.000
8 In my work I like to feel I am making some effort, not just for myself but for the organization	4.24	4.45	−3.13	0.002
9 The offer of a bit more money with another employer would not seriously make me think of changing my job	3.18	3.49	−2.79	0.005
Commitment index	34	35	−1.31	0.190
Alpha coefficient	0.84	0.60		
K-R8 coefficient	0.88	0.70		

Note: For each item there was a five-point answer scale ranging from 'definitely true' to 'definitely false', and the responses were coded in such a manner that a higher score indicates a higher degree of commitment.

Consequences of employees' commitment for organizational structure

Hypothesis 8: Control systems in Indian organizations will be more relaxed than those in their English counterparts.

This hypothesis was advanced on the speculation that Indian employees would have a higher degree of commitment to their organizations than would the English employees. Since this was not the case, and the two samples scored almost the same on the commitment index, one would now expect, still maintaining a culturalist perspective, that control strategies in the two groups of organizations would be similar. This was in fact the case, as will be discussed in the following section, in conjunction with the implication of trust for organizational structure.

4. Interpersonal trust and organization (Hypotheses 9 and 10)

Employees' state of interpersonal trust

Hypothesis 9: On the whole the state of trust among both Indian and English employees will be the same.

There were nine items in the questionnaire to measure the extent to which employees trusted each other. Four of the items had been adopted with modifications from Cook and Wall (1980). Table 8.12 shows responses to these items. The internal reliability tests showed a high consistency among the items and they could be collectively treated as a composite measure. A trust index for each country was computed by aggregating the individual scores for the nine items. The possible range was from 9 to 45. Both samples scored 34 on the index (figures are rounded). Hypothesis 9 is not rejected.

Consequences of employees' state of interpersonal trust for organizational structure

Hypothesis 10: Control strategies in English and Indian organizations will be similar.

The control strategies employed in the two groups of organizations were indeed similar, albeit for most part for non-cultural reasons: in both countries managers and other members of staff were treated differently from shop floor manual workers and lower-grade clerical employees. Control over the former was far more relaxed than over the latter. The performance of the former was monitored through target setting and reporting, and that of the latter through time keeping and daily and/or other frequent periodical productivity checks.

The differences between the control policies employed for the two groups of employees in each sample is also consistent with the argument advanced in hypotheses 11 and 12 (Chapter 7, Table 7.4) which were based on the class conflict between management and workers in the two countries. Since this aspect of the study is more closely related to political economic factors, it will be discussed in detail in the next chapter, where the implications of some 'non-cultural' factors for the participating organizations are examined.

Table 8.12 *Trust*

Items	English (mean)	Indian (mean)	Value of 't'	Level of confidence (p)
1 Most of my colleagues can be relied upon to carry out what they say they will do*	3.74	3.53	2.68	0.007
2 Most people in this organization are honest and can be trusted	3.99	3.66	3.96	0.000
3 Most of the employees here have a strong sense of responsibility	3.46	3.49	−0.35	0.730
4 Employees here can be trusted to work hard for the good of the organization	3.43	3.83	−5.07	0.000
5 I have full confidence in the abilities of my subordinates to carry out their work	3.73	3.93	−2.68	0.008
6 I have no confidence in the good intentions of my subordinates to their work	4.04	4.17	−1.57	0.118
7 Most of my colleagues would work just as hard even when their bosses are not around*	3.75	3.78	−0.25	0.800
8 Most employees here would on occasion be prepared to take advantage if they had a chance to deceive others	3.62	3.57	0.56	0.578
9 Employees here can be trusted to provide management with correct information about what they are doing	3.87	3.91	−0.57	0.567
Trust index	34	34	−0.69	0.489
Alpha coefficient	0.81	0.78		
K-R8 coefficient	0.85	0.83		

Notes: For each item there was a five-point answer scale ranging from 'definitely true' to 'definitely false', and the responses were coded in such a manner that a higher score indicates a higher degree of tolerance for ambiguity.

* These items are adopted with modification from Cook and Wall's 'trust' scale.

5. Expectations from a job and organization (Hypotheses 13, 14, 15, 16)

Employees' expectations from a job

This section of the questionnaire consisted of eight items which were devised following Maslow's concept of need hierarchy (1954). Table 8.13 shows these items and the responses given by the respondents to each of them. Table 8.14 shows the rank order of each of these

Table 8.13 Expectations from job

Items	English			Indian			Value of 't'	Level of confidence (p)
	Important (%)	Not important (%)	Mean score	Important (%)	Not important (%)	Mean score		
How important would it be to you to:								
Have a job that is very secure	72.3	2.7	3.92	59.7	11.4	3.67	3.49	0.001
Get to know other people while on the job	52.8	10.1	3.56	62.6	14.3	3.62	−0.76	0.445
Have a good pay and fringe benefits	78.1	2.1	4.04	67.1	5.7	3.86	2.75	0.006
Belong to a social group at work	10.3	55.9	2.36	36.7	27.7	3.09	−8.89	0.000
Have considerable freedom and independence in how you do your job	71.9	3.0	3.88	77.2	8.2	4.01	−1.80	0.072
Learn new things	78.6	2.1	4.06	92.7	2.1	4.40	−5.94	0.000
Have status and prestige in your job and have your friends and colleagues respect you	48.0	12.5	3.44	74.8	7.2	4.00	−7.75	0.000
Have opportunities to use your initiative and be creative and imaginative	81.2	4.2	4.06	87.1	3.0	4.28	−3.49	0.001

Note: For each item there was a five-point answer scale ranging from 'of utmost importance' to 'of little or no importance', and the responses were coded in such a manner that a higher score indicates a higher importance placed on the item.

Cultural and organizational assessment

Table 8.14 *Expectations from job – rank order*

	English (rank order)	Indian (rank order)
1 Job security	4	6
2 Get to know others	6	7
3 Good pay and fringe benefits	3	5
4 Belong to a group	8	8
5 Freedom and independence	5	3
6 Learn new things	1	1
7 Status and prestige	7	4
8 Be creative	1	2

features in terms of the importance of their presence in the job. The two features which were of most importance to English employees were 'being creative and imaginative at work' and 'having an opportunity to learn new things' – a mean score of 4.06 for both. These were closely followed by 'a good pay' (4.04) and 'job security' (3.92). 'Having freedom and independence' ranked fourth – mean score of 3.88. The least important feature of the job was 'belonging to a group'.

To Indian respondents the most important feature of a job was 'having an opportunity to learn new things' (4.40). It was followed by 'being creative and imaginative at work' (4.28), 'having freedom and independence' (4.01), and 'status and prestige' (4.00). 'Belonging to a group' was of least importance to the Indian employees, but they gave it significantly greater importance than did their English counterparts.

Hypothesis 13: Autonomy and freedom at work will be of higher importance to English employees than will be to the Indian employees.

Hypothesis 15: Good pay and other financial benefits will be of less importance to Indian employees than to English employees.

As Tables 8.13 and 8.14 show, freedom and independence were more important to Indian employees (rank 3) than to the English employees (rank 5). Hypothesis 13 is not therefore supported. Good pay and fringe benefits were more important to English employees (rank 3) than to the Indian employees (rank 5). Hypothesis 15 was not rejected.

From the comparison of the two groups three points stand out. First, the job features which are important to one group are, to some extent, different from the ones which are important to the other. To Indian employees the so-called intrinsic aspects of a job – learning new things, having freedom and independence, and status and prestige – are of more importance than the so-called extrinsic ones; to the English employees a mixture of both – learning new things, being creative, good pay, job security, and having freedom and independence – was important. Secondly, those items which are considered important to the Indian employees are scored higher than the English employees score their important items; and a greater proportion of the former indicated the items as being important, than is the case for the latter. For instance, 'learning new things' is ranked first by both groups. The Indians scored 4.40 on this item; the English scored lower, 4.06. And 92.7 percent of the Indian employees in comparison with 78.6 percent of the English employees said that to them this item was of importance. The same is true for all other items.

Finally, if the responses given to these items can be interpreted as a reflection of the respondents' need hierarchy (in a Maslowian sense), the results of this section of the study support the author's hypothesis about the influence of culture on employees' need hierarchy and challenges the universality of Maslow's model. The author would also like to draw attention to the findings of her similar research in Iran (Tayeb, 1979) as yet another case in which Maslow's theory of hierarchy of needs failed to gain support.

Consequences of employees' expectations from a job for organizational structure

Hypothesis 14: Authority and decision making power are delegated lower down the hierarchy in English organizations compared to their Indian counterparts.

As was noted earlier, on the whole there was more delegation of authority in English organizations than there was in their Indian counterparts. The Mann–Whitney test showed that the difference between the two samples, although not significant, was worthy of note ($p = 0.08$). Hypothesis 14 is therefore not wholly rejected.

Hypothesis 16: Reward and punishment policies will be more financially oriented in English organizations than in their Indian counterparts.

In all the participating organizations rewards took financial and non-financial forms and were linked to performance. However, in the Indian organizations the punishment strategies adopted for manual workers were non-financial only and generally mild, such as shortening annual holidays and failure to promote. Because the government's regulations aim at maintaining employment and minimum living standards for this group of employees, the managers would not be allowed, for instance, to dismiss manual workers or reduce their wages under any circumstances, even if they committed gross misconduct and breach of contract. The rewards for managers and other white-collar staff usually took, for tax purposes, non-monetary forms, such as a company house and car. Hypothesis 16 is supported for the English sample but not for the Indian sample.

6. Attitudes to management practices and organization (Hypotheses 17 and 18)

Employees' attitudes toward management practices

Hypothesis 17: English employees will have a more egalitarian outlook towards management practices and favour a participative style compared to the Indian employees.

This section consisted of eight items (in four pairs) which had been adopted from Haire et al. (1966). The items were based on contrasting assumptions between 'modern' and 'classical' theories of the nature of employees and the management of organizations. Each item was related to one set of assumptions or attitudes on which the two types of theories differ, and together the items covered four areas: attitudes about others, information sharing, participation, and control systems. A high score for each item indicates attitudes in favour of modern participative management practices, and a low score the traditional directive ones. Table 8.15 shows the responses to these items.

The two groups were significantly different from one another on four items. Indian employees had more negative views about an average human being's willingness to accept responsibility, believed more that leaders should give their subordinates detailed instructions and only the information which was necessary to carry out their immediate tasks, but they also thought it was better for all the employees concerned to participate more in decision making. The Indian employees' responses to the first three items contradict their answers to the question about participation for all. Indian respondents perhaps paid 'lip service' to participative management styles.

Consequences of employees' attitudes to management practices for organizational structure

Hypothesis 18: There will be more consultation and communication in English organizations compared to their Indian counterparts.

Table 8.15 *Attitudes to management practices*

Items	English (mean)	Indian (mean)	Value of 't'	Level of confidence (p)
Pair 1 Attitudes about others				
The average human being prefers to be directed, wishes to avoid responsibility, and has relatively little ambition	3.25	2.94	3.37	0.001
Leadership skills can be acquired by most people regardless of their particular inborn traits and abilities	2.85	2.92	−0.86	0.393
Average mean values on the pair	3.05	2.94		
Pair 2 Information sharing				
A good leader should give detailed and complete instructions to his subordinates rather than giving them merely general directions and depending upon their initiative to work out the details	2.75	2.19	5.89	0.000
A superior should give his subordinates only that information which is necessary for them to do their immediate tasks	3.62	2.73	9.87	0.000
Average mean values on the pair	3.16	2.46		
Pair 3 Attitudes towards participation				
In the work situation, if subordinates cannot influence me then I lose some influence over them	2.81	2.74	0.90	0.366
It is better to have all the people concerned to participate in decision making rather than the boss making decisions on his own*	3.45	3.65	−2.27	0.024
Average mean values on the pair	3.13	3.19		
Pair 4 Attitudes towards type of control system				
The use of financial rewards (pay, promotion, etc.) and punishment (failure to promote, etc.) is not the best way to get subordinates to work	3.29	3.21	0.93	0.351
The superior's authority over his subordinates in an organization is primarily economic	2.98	2.85	1.68	0.093
Average mean values on the pair	3.13	3.03		

Notes: For each item there was a five-point answer scale ranging from 'strongly agree' to 'strongly disagree', and the responses were coded in such a manner that a higher score indicates a higher endorsement of democratic values.

* This item is a modification of Haire et al.'s (1966) original statement.

Five items relating to the pattern of communication amongst employees and between employees and people from outside the organization were included in the survey questionnaire. Table 8.16 illustrates the responses given to these items. A constant feature of English organizations is that their employees communicate with their superiors, subordinates, colleagues and people in other departments to a greater extent compared to their Indian counterparts. The English employees' higher scores on communication can be a reflection of their culturally-rooted democratic values and interest in participation, consultation, discussion and collective action. The Indian employees' lower scores are consistent with the Indian people's authoritarian culture, where decisions are generally made by seniors with little consultation (e.g. arranged marriages), and submission is expected from juniors (Meade, 1967; Kakar, 1971a and 1971b).

DISCUSSION

Culture and work-related attitudes

There are systematic differences between English and Indian employees in some of the work-related attitudes measured in the study. These are: attitudes to power and authority, tolerance for ambiguity, expectations from a job and satisfaction with organization, and attitudes toward management practices. Some of the differences between the two samples are consistent with the cultural backgrounds of the respondents. Chapter 7 showed that in comparison with the English, Indian people in general are: more obedient to their seniors, are less able to cope with new and uncertain situations, are more fatalistic, and, when in a position of authority, are less willing to take account of other people's opinions. These cultural characteristics appear to have been reflected, respectively, in the Indian employees' lower perception of power, lower tolerance for ambiguity, higher satisfaction with their work organization, and more traditional directive attitudes to management practices, compared to the English employees.

Some of the differences between the two samples in the expectations from a job do not seem to be directly related to the differences between their respective cultures. English people value independence and autonomy far more than do the Indians. But the Indian employees whose work attitudes were studied here attached greater importance to having autonomy at work than did the English employees. This could be because of the English employees' greater actual autonomy and discretion at work compared to the Indian employees. In the former the need for autonomy may have been

Cultures and organizational structure 131

Table 8.16 *Communication pattern*

	English (mean)	Indian (mean)	Value of 't'	Level of confidence (p)
1 Communication with boss	2.40	2.21	1.90	0.058
2 Communication with subordinates	3.03	2.52	4.48	0.000
3 Communication with colleagues in one's own area of work	3.39	2.36	10.30	0.000
4 Communication with people from other areas of work	2.34	2.03	3.24	0.001
5 Communication with people from outside the organization	1.96	2.24	−2.52	0.012

Note: There was a five point answer scale for each item ranging from 'much of my time' to 'very little of my time', and the responses were coded in such a manner that a higher score indicates a higher time spent on communication.

relatively more satisfied and was therefore of less importance compared to the latter. Organizational culture, as distinct from societal culture, may be an influencing factor here.

There is some degree of similarity between the two samples in individualism, commitment, and interpersonal trust. These similarities are consistent with the respondents' cultural backgrounds in some cases, and inconsistent in others. Chapter 7 argued that the English in general are individualistic, their commitment is to themselves and their immediate family, and that they are a trustworthy and trusting people. The English employees' relatively high scores on individualism and interpersonal trust and low scores on commitment to their work organization are consistent with their cultural upbringing.

Indian people, in contrast, are collectivist. They have a strong commitment to their immediate family and the scope of their commitment is much wider and includes all their relatives, friends and religious community. This characteristic does not appear to be reflected in the Indian employees' scores for individualism and commitment, indicating that work organization is not a part of the in-group to which they have a strong commitment. 'Non-cultural' factors, such as organizational climate, political economic conditions, and employees' hierarchical positions, may account for this finding. Some of these factors will be discussed in the next chapter.

It should be noted that the inconsistencies observed between the respondents' cultural backgrounds and some of their work-related attitudes exist only in the Indian sample. This may be, among other things, because of the influence of British style of within-organization relationships on the Indian employees, as a consequence of the colonial links between the two countries. As Shenoy (1981) points out, under the British Raj India received a steady injection of British bureaucratic methods over a period of 200 years.

Work-related attitudes and organizational structure

The two groups of organizations are different from one another in delegation, formalization, and communication patterns, and are similar in centralization, joint decisions, specialization and control strategies.

English managers delegated their decision-making power lower down the hierarchy than did the Indian managers. The Indian employees, not surprisingly, perceived themselves to have less autonomy in doing their job than did their English counterparts. The higher degree of delegation in English organizations is consistent with their employees' higher perception of autonomy and their cultural upbringing. The lower degree of delegation in the Indian organizations, however, sits ill with their employees' expectations for greater autonomy at work. These expectations, it seems, are ignored by Indian managers. This is consistent with the Indian people's lower willingness to take account of others' views, and their authoritarian power relationships.

The participating organizations' scores on formalization were found unrelated to their employees' tolerance of ambiguity, as hypothesized in Chapter 7. However, this dimension appears to reflect another aspect of the employees' respective cultures – love of privacy and independence in the case of the English, and lack of concern for privacy and space in the case of the Indians.

The differing patterns of communication in the two groups of organization are consistent with the differences in their employees' attitudes to management practices. English employees held more modern and participative attitudes toward managerial issues, and tended to communicate with each other and to seek each other's opinions to a larger extent; the Indian employees held more directive and non-participative views, and tended to consult one another to a lesser extent.

The similarities between English and Indian organizations in centralization and specialization appear to be more consistent with the similar technical and task-environmental factors that they shared in common, rather than their employees' work-related attitudes.

The control strategies employed by the managers of the participating organizations were similar across the two countries. In neither case did these strategies reflect the cultural attitudes of their respective peoples. Rather, they reflected their employees' level of commitment to their work organizations, which in turn were a consequence of the class conflicts between management and workers that exist within their societies as industrial nations.

The results of the study discussed so far lend only partial support to the culturalist perspective. To the extent that these results can be generalized, this perspective may be said to offer a useful but incomplete explanation for the English and Indian organizations studied here. The organization–culture model that was hypothesized in Chapters 5 and 7 on the basis of the arguments of the culturalist writers (Tables 5.1 and 7.4), while apparently accounting for some of the links between culture and work-related attitudes, and between organizational structure and work-related attitudes, does not allow for the absence of other expected links. There is clearly a need to look for non-cultural factors which may enhance our understanding of the organizations investigated. These points will be dealt with in more detail in Chapter 9.

9
Non-Cultural Influences on Work Attitudes and Organizational Structure

The previous chapter argued that culture could not explain some of the similarities and differences between the English and Indian organizations which participated in the study and between their employees' work-related attitudes. The present chapter explores some of the non-cultural factors which may have accounted for these similarities and differences. (See Tayeb, 1984, for tables of statistics.)

WORK-RELATED ATTITUDES AND SOME NON-CULTURAL FACTORS

It has been argued that factors such as wealth, occupation, education, age, sex, and race influence people's values and attitudes (Haire et al., 1966; Rokeach, 1979; Hofstede, 1980). The impact of some of these factors, especially occupation, education and age, were examined for the present samples' work-related attitudes. Employees' age did not seem to have any significant and systematic impact on their attitudes, except on tolerance of ambiguity and on commitment, but occupation and education in many cases did.

Power and authority

Analysis of variance and the Pearson correlation tests suggested in both countries a strong association between employees' position in the hierarchy and their perception of power within their organization. English managers perceived themselves to have more power than other employees in their organization: they were more prepared to argue with people in higher positions, had more opportunity to have a say in decision making, had easier access to their boss, believed less that people in authority were more intelligent and knowledgeable, and were less afraid to disagree with their boss than most other employees.

In the Indian sample there were differences between various occupational categories in various items. The pattern of response, however, was not systematic and was in some cases even contradictory. They indicated a higher perception of power by managers on some items in comparison with some employees, and a lower perception on other items in comparison with others. An interesting point to note was that Indian manual workers were less afraid to disagree with their bosses, and less obedient to them than were other employees, even the managers. A likely explanation for this lies in the relatively powerful position enjoyed by the organized workers in India, encouraged by pro-union legislation, compared to white-collar employees. The Indian organizations which participated in the present study were all unionized.

The impact of education on employees' perception of power was to a lesser extent than that of occupation, and was less systematic. The English employees with higher degrees believed less that obedience and respect for authority were virtues, and less still that good employees did not contradict their boss. Those with a lower level of education thought that employees should receive equal salaries regardless of their hierarchical position.

In the Indian sample various educational groups were significantly different from one another on only one item: in comparison with the highly educated employees, those with lower levels of education believed more that people in authority were knowledgeable and intelligent.

On the whole, level of education differentiated more between occupational groups in the English sample than it did in the Indian sample. This may have been caused by the nature of the educational systems in the two countries. In England, the system encourages a smaller power 'gap' and a more egalitarian authority relationship; in India, the opposite is generally the case. It is therefore plausible to suggest that a higher level of education in England, other things being equal, results in a greater exposure to egalitarian relationships and consequently a higher perception of power; whereas in India a higher level of education may not have the same effect.

Tolerance of ambiguity

English employees' tolerance of ambiguity was higher than that of the Indian employees when occupation was controlled for; but the interesting point is that in both countries, managers, specialists and engineers/technicians had higher levels of tolerance of ambiguity than their lower-rank colleagues, such as supervisors, office workers and shop floor manual employees. This indicates a strong influence by the kind of job that the respondents performed, as well as their cultural backgrounds, on their ability to tolerate and cope with uncertainty. The senior employees carried out jobs which involved greater opportunity to make decisions, to handle uncertainty, and to take risks; whereas the latter's jobs were simple and routine with fewer opportunities to face uncertainty.

The English employees' tolerance of ambiguity increased significantly as their level of education increased, but this association was not the case for the Indian employees. This, again, may have something to do with the different types of teaching practices that are employed in the two countries. The English educational practices are based largely on self-experimentation, trial and error, and self-discovery, a system which encourages facing up to and coping with uncertainty and ambiguity. In the Indian educational system, the teaching practices are mainly based on reading and memorizing textbooks, a system which does not encourage coping with uncertainty.

Age had a similar relationship with tolerance of ambiguity in both countries – younger employees had a much higher tolerance of uncertainty than did their older colleagues.

Commitment

Managers in both countries scored higher on commitment than did other employees. The difference between this group and the manual workers was the largest in both samples. This is hardly surprising, given the different treatment the two groups of employees received from their employers. In both countries, the managers and other white-collar employees had greater advantages over the manual workers in many respects, such as power, status, pay, physical working conditions, eating places, rules for lunch and tea breaks, and holidays. Shop floor workers in both countries were subject to a tighter control at work. They had to clock in and out at specific times, and in some of the companies which produced chemicals and drugs, were subject to physical search every time they left the company premises.

The differences between shop floor workers and white-collar employees, especially managers, inside the participating organizations appear to be a reflection of the social structures and systems of their respective societies. In England managers consider themselves members of the middle class, which shares in the ownership and participates in the control of the means of production, and manual workers see themselves as members of the working class, exploited by the former. In most cases, the relationship between management and workers is ridden with mistrust and hostility, emanating from a conflict of interests between the two classes.

In India, in addition to the industrial class conflict, the caste membership further exacerbates the generally hostile relationship between managers and workers. The former belong to higher castes, and the latter are largely recruited from among lower-caste villagers and slum dwellers of the urban areas. In both countries, older employees had a greater commitment to their work organizations than their younger colleagues.

Trust

There were significant differences between various occupational groups in each sample in their degree of trust, but these differences were not systematically related to the positions of the respondents. Level of education and age had no bearing on trust.

Individualism

There was virtually no difference between English occupational groups in their degree of individualism, but there were significant differences between these groups in the Indian sample. The employees in the higher positions were more individualistic than their junior colleagues.

Chapter 8 reported unexpectedly high scores for Indian employees on the individualism items. These scores were noted to be inconsistent with their cultural background. This inconsistency appears to have been caused by their occupational positions.

In neither country was employees' degree of individualism influenced to any significant extent by their level of education and age.

Expectations from the job

In both countries, employees' occupational position had a significant influence on some of their expectations from the job. English supervisors and manual workers attached more importance to job security than did other groups. This is to be expected, given the economic conditions in Britain at the time the survey was carried out, when manual employees especially were being made redundant on a massive scale. The shop floor workers attached the least importance to having an opportunity to be creative at work compared to their other colleagues. This may be because the routine manual jobs that most of these employees performed had affected their predispositions. It may also be that manual work had attracted those who did not want a responsible creative job.

In the Indian sample, 'a good pay' and 'status, prestige and respect' were more important to manual workers than to other groups. This is not surprising. This group of employees were paid very low wages and were the least respected people within their work organizations, mainly because of their low caste. The shop floor workers also attached a greater importance to job security compared to other employees. This may be because of the abundance of (especially unskilled) manual workers in the Indian labour market which gives them less security and confidence in finding an alternative job.

Job security was also more important to the less educated respondents in India than it was to the more educated ones. The job market in the country is very competitive. One of the major criteria on which employees are recruited is their educational qualifications. For example, for a simple secretarial job applicants are required to have at least a first or an upper second class honours degree from a good university (my sources are job advertisements published in the Indian press). The Indian managers whom the author interviewed said that most of their supervisors had at least a first degree in an engineering discipline.

Attitudes to management practices

In both samples there were some differences between various occupational groups in their attitudes to management practices. On the whole, the employees in higher positions tended more to favour non-financial reward and punishment and believed less in other people's willingness to accept responsibility and ability to learn leadership skills, compared to those in lower-ranked jobs. An interesting point to note is that English managers were in favour of information sharing to a greater extent not only compared to their own colleagues but also to their counterparts in India.

Finally, a discriminant analysis was carried out in order to examine further the strength of employees' non-cultural backgrounds in relation to their cultural upbringing in influencing their work-related attitudes. The test showed that the attitudes measured in the study classified correctly 97.47 percent of the respondents by their country of origin, 73.68 percent by education, 68.80 percent by occupation, and 67.91 percent by age. This suggests that culture has a stronger impact on work-related attitudes than do other social factors.

So far the findings of the study suggest that employees' work-related attitudes are not only influenced by their cultural backgrounds (in the ideational sense), but also by their hierarchical position inside and outside their work organization, level of education and age, and by the political economic environments of their respective country. Some of these factors are common to more than one society and their combined effect may increase the similarities between comparable categories of employees. For instance, India and

England are two industrialized nations, and also because of their past colonial links, their economies are characterized by similar class conflicts and hostile industrial relations. The present study suggests that these factors have similar implications for employees' and their managers' attitudes and behaviours. In both countries, manual workers had a much lower level of commitment to their organization than did the employees in higher positions, especially managers. Similarly, in both countries, the managers, in response to this situation, had employed a dual control system: a tight and direct control policy for manual workers and a more relaxed and indirect one for managers and other members of staff.

The study suggests that power is a complex and dynamic concept and there can be no single determinant for it. People may perceive themselves to have different degrees of power within their work organization, and indeed elsewhere, depending on the particular situations in which they find themselves. This may explain, among other things, why there was no consistency among both the 'power distance' and 'perceived power' items, and between the respondents' scores on the individual items in the two measures.

ORGANIZATIONAL STRUCTURE AND SOME NON-CULTURAL FACTORS

Chapter 8 noted that English and Indian organizations scored similarly on centralization, joint decisions, specialization, and chief executive's span of control, but differently on other aspects. The chapter explored some of the cultural explanations for these similarities and differences. The following sections examine some relevant non-cultural and task-environmental factors.

Centralization

Although the two samples scored similarly on this dimension, a closer examination of the scale and other measures related to it reveals some interesting differences between the two samples.

First, a breakdown of the items comprising the scale, following Yassai-Ardekani (1979), shows that on the whole English organizations were more centralized on financial decisions and less so on operative decisions compared to their Indian counterparts. This, on the one hand, may reflect the financial hardship and more competitive environments that the English organizations were experiencing at the time the study was conducted. This might have caused the managers to tighten their grip over financial and strategic decisions.

In the Indian case, on the other hand, their higher centralization of operative decisions reflects their own industrial relations climate. Most of the operative decisions concern appointment, promotion and dismissal of shop floor employees. Indian government regulations are very stringent and pro-worker in this respect. For example, managers cannot easily dismiss workers or punish them in any way even if they breach their terms of contract. Workers' representatives are very powerful in negotiating promotion and wage increases and other working conditions. If a manager wishes to promote or reward a worker, he may have to do the same for all his workmates. The senior managers therefore are very careful as to who should be recruited, promoted or dismissed, and they are personally involved in the decisions concerning these matters.

Secondly, in both countries, expenditure of money on capital items was more centralized than on revenue items, and the expenditure of unallocated money was more centralized than allocated money. This strongly suggests the operation of a contingent factor, namely *perceived risk*, attached to the decision, including its having longer term consequences.

Specialization

The two samples scored similarly on this dimension. Here, too, one must note a few points. First, although the aggregate scores on specialization were similar, the specialized functions were different. For instance, in the Indian company in the chemicals pair, environmental pollution and medical matters were dealt with by a specialized department, whereas the English counterpart had a specialized section for its printing and publishing requirements.

Secondly, some of the firms had contracted out some of their functions, but their counterparts had not. Thirdly, some of the English organizations which were part of a parent group, had some of their functions performed at the group headquarters or central pools, but their Indian counterparts performed these themselves.

Fourthly, all the English firms, except the brewery and confectionery companies, had specialized departments for R & D activities to meet, in the words of their managers, their competitors' challenge; whereas none of the Indian firms felt the need for such a specialist function, mainly because they did not face any serious competition. At the most, they would send their senior officers to attend international exhibitions and conferences in order to learn and come back with new ideas.

Formalization

Indian organizations scored considerably lower on this dimension than did their English counterparts. A reason for this, apart from cultural differences, may be that the Aston formalization scale employed in the present study did not adequately reflect the degree of procedural control in the organizations investigated. The scale measures the extent to which *written documents* are used in the companies. There may have also been unwritten rules and directives which regulated employees' activities. This may have been especially so in the Indian organizations where most of the shop floor manual workers were illiterate – a political economy-type factor.

Moreover, formalization is, in fact, a means to control employees and to improve their performance (Child, 1984a). There are other ways in which control can be exerted. The managers who participated in the study mentioned a variety of methods that they employed, such as training courses, personal supervision, time-keeping, and verbal contact. My discussions with these managers suggest that the Indian managers employed direct supervision and personal contact with shop floor employees as well as their immediate subordinates to a larger extent than did the English managers.

Communication

English employees spent more time on communication than the Indian employees. This is not only consistent with the cultural differences between the two nations, but also with their respective political economic environments. Many of the English firms had a much smaller share of the market compared to their Indian counterparts. This was to a great extent a direct result of their respective governments' economic policies. Although the economic system in both countries is based on a capitalistic mode of production with both private and public enterprises, Indian capitalism is much more protectionist and the government intervenes in the economy much more directly. For example, local industries are protected against foreign competition by the government's strict import policies. The present Conservative government in England, in contrast, pursues an 'open door' policy and has dismantled import controls. As a consequence, manufacturing companies face fierce competition from foreign firms.

In short, Indian organizations, with their more stable environment, spent less time on communication and consultation than did the English organizations with their less stable environment.

A second way of testing the influence of non-cultural factors on the participating organizations was to compare the two samples' context-

Table 9.1 Correlations between structural dimensions and contextual factors (for each country separately)

	Technological change	Size	Status	Ownership	Control	Age	Market share
Centralization:							
English	0.62*	0.15	−0.02	0.29	0.23	−0.15	0.21
Indian	0.61*	−0.29	−0.33	−0.14	0.30	−0.28	0.67
Difference:	ns	ns	ns	ns	ns	ns	ns
Delegation:							
English	−0.11	0.82††	0.34	0.40	0.29	−0.30	0.05
Indian	−0.33	0.46	−0.29	0.10	−0.02	−0.74**	−0.65
Difference:	ns	ns	ns	ns	ns	s	s
Joint decisions:							
English	0.41	−0.21	−0.09	−0.07	0.11	0.18	−0.65
Indian	−0.13	−0.67**	0.03	−0.70**	−0.89††	0.51	−0.33
Difference:	ns	ns	ns	s	s	ns	ns
Formalization:							
English	0.30	−0.47	−0.51	−0.20	0.18	0.55	0.50
Indian	−0.08	−0.47	0.50	−0.63	−0.28	−0.05	0.61
Difference:	ns	ns	s	ns	ns	ns	ns
Specialization:							
English	0.82††	0.56	0.49	0.78†	0.75**	−0.47	0.61
Indian	0.28	0.66**	−0.30	−0.30	0.40	−0.38	−0.01
Difference:	s	ns	ns	s	ns	ns	s
Chief executive's span of control:							
English	0.15	−0.76**	−0.18	−0.27	−0.38	0.00	−0.58
Indian	0.39	0.12	−0.19	0.04	0.37	−0.46	−0.54
Difference:	ns	s	ns	ns	ns	ns	ns

Non-cultural influences on organizational structure 143

Number of hierarchical levels:							
English	0.43	0.60	0.00	0.38	0.55	−0.10	−0.19
Indian	0.66**	0.23	−0.45	0.28	0.65**	−0.23	0.42
Difference:	ns	ns	ns	ns	ns	ns	ns
Communication with boss:							
English	0.90††	0.25	0.26	0.51	0.65**	−0.32	−0.54
Indian	0.00	−0.15	0.31	−0.24	0.07	0.66**	−0.30
Difference:	s	ns	ns	s	s	s	ns
Communication with subordinates:							
English	0.18	0.07	0.29	−0.18	0.04	0.38	0.00
Indian	−0.13	0.30	−0.38	0.33	−0.17	0.19	−0.82†
Difference:	ns	ns	ns	ns	ns	ns	s
Communication with colleagues:							
English	0.07	0.19	−0.49	−0.17	0.10	0.47	−0.15
Indian	0.63	0.39	−0.84††	0.60	0.43	0.05	−0.40
Difference:	s	ns	s	s	ns	ns	ns
Communication with people from other areas of work:							
English	0.51	0.27	−0.64	0.56	0.69**	−0.38	0.17
Indian	0.30	0.59	0.04	0.68**	0.75**	−0.62	0.54
Difference:	ns	ns	s	ns	ns	ns	ns
Communication with people from outside the organization:							
English	−0.50	0.39	−0.01	−0.25	−0.17	0.19	0.00
Indian	−0.15	−0.19	0.19	−0.21	0.22	−0.40	0.57
Difference:	ns	ns	ns	ns	ns	ns	s

Note: * = $p < 0.10$, ** = $p < 0.05$, † = $p < 0.01$, †† = $p < 0.001$, ns = not significant, s = significant. Reproduced from *Organization Studies* 8/3, 1987.

structure relations. In order to do this a Pearson correlation test between structural and contextual variables was carried out for each sample separately. The small number of cases in the correlation test for each country means that only the correlations with very high coefficients are significant. Also the results should be treated as tentative and suggestive. However, as was argued in Chapter 5, the careful control for the contextual variables of the two samples should enhance the credibility of the results. Table 9.1 shows the results of this test. It shows there are both similarities and differences between the two groups of organizations in their context–structure relationships.

Similarities
The correlations which are high and consistent in both countries are (a) between technological change and centralization ($p<0.10$) and (b) between ownership/control and communication with people from other sections of the organization ($p<0.05$). The positive correlation between technological change and the degree of centralization indicates that the more innovations there are in the technology used by a firm, the more likely it is that the firm's senior management will keep decisions in their own hands, at the top. This appears to contradict the assumptions of many contingency theorists in this respect. It has been generally argued that organizations with complex and changing technologies tend to be more decentralized (e.g. Schoonhoven, 1981).

However, the present results may still be interpreted as a support for a contingency theory-type argument. It is plausible to argue that the uncertainty and competition in the market caused by a rapid technological change may make senior managers more sensitive to technological matters and want to be more directly involved in decisions about technology. They may even, with the help of new technology, want to centralize information processing, thereby enhancing their control over decisions (Child, 1984a).

As for the correlation between ownership and control and communication with people from outside the organization, given the coding procedures for ownership and control variables, the positive correlation means that in the firms which are owned by general public shareholders and managed by salaried managers, employees interact with people from outside to a larger extent than do those working for the firms which are run by owner-managers.

There are some other correlations which, although they are not statistically significant in both samples at the same time, are nevertheless interesting. The direction of some of these supports some of the contingency theory arguments. For instance, in both countries the larger the firm is, the more senior managers delegate their authority down the hierarchy, the more they create specialized functions, the longer is their vertical span of control, and the more employees spend time on communication with each other. Similarly, in both countries the firms with a higher rate of technological change have a higher degree of functional specialization. The direction of some of the correlations in both countries are opposite to the contingency theorists' predictions. For instance, formalization in both countries is negatively correlated with size (see Marsh and Mannari, 1981 as an example of the evidence to the contrary). As was argued earlier, this dimension seems to be associated more with the organizations' cultural and political economic environments than with their task-specific contexts.

Differences
There are many differences between the two samples in the associations between their contextual variables and structural dimensions, both in magnitude and in direction, and these differences are statistically significant in sixteen cases. The significant correlations are discussed below for each sample separately.

English sample Size is correlated positively with delegation and negatively with chief executive's span of control. This means that in larger organizations senior managers delegate their authority lower down the hierarchy and, not unexpectedly, have a smaller span of control. Technological change and ownership and control have positive correlations with specialization and communication with the boss. This indicates that the firms which experience a higher rate of change in their technology and those which are owned by general public shareholders and managed by salaried managers, have more of their functions performed by specialized departments and/or persons. Employees in these firms communicate with their subordinates to a larger extent than do those in the other firms.

Market share is positively correlated with the chief executive's span of control: the larger the market share, the larger is the span of control. If a large share in the market is taken to mean a less competitive and more stable environment, senior managers of the firms operating in this kind of environment may be expected to make relatively fewer non-routine decisions. These managers are therefore able to supervise directly more functional departments and have more departmental managers to report to them.

Status has a negative correlation with communication with people outside the organization. Given the coding procedures for the variable status, this means that the employees of the firms which are subsidiaries of a parent group communicate less with people from outside their company. This is also reflected in the pattern of functional specialization of these organizations as discussed earlier. Some of the functions which required direct dealings with the people and institutions outside the company, such as legal and insurance activities, were either contracted out in these companies or carried out by the parent group.

This pattern of correlations is highly consistent with the contingency model predictions about context–structure relationships.

Indian sample The pattern of correlations for the Indian data is mixed: some support the contingency model, some reject it. Size is correlated positively with specialization and negatively with joint decisions. This means that larger organizations have more specialized functions, and their senior managers make fewer decisions jointly with their subordinates. Ownership and control have positive correlations with joint decisions – the senior managers of the firms which are owned by public shareholders and managed by professionals make fewer decisions in conjunction with subordinates and their employees communicate more with people from outside.

Age and market share have negative correlation with delegation. This means that in the younger firms and those with smaller market share, where environment is more competitive and more unstable, senior managers delegate their authority lower down the hierarchy. It must be pointed out that the younger Indian firms are those which are owned by public shareholders and are managed by professional managers. Their higher degree of delegation therefore may also be a reflection of their familiarity with modern management practices.

The study strongly suggests that task-related and other non-cultural factors have significant implications for the structures of the participating organizations. This is further highlighted when one examines the results of the attitudes and the organizational structural surveys more closely. Although many of the employees' work-related attitudes were found to be influenced by their cultural upbringing, there were some which were not. These were more influenced by the industrial and political environment and other national institutions in their respective countries.

Many of the hypothesized 'linkages' between work-related attitudes and organizational aspects were refuted. The study lends support to both contingency and political economy models in this respect. However, there are some findings that do not fit in either of these models. For instance, although the organizations were matched in pairs on almost all of their contextual variables, their structural dimensions were not similar in all cases across the two countries. The cultural perspective model appears to be more successful in explaining these dissimilarities.

There were also some instances of an interaction between, and combined influences of, cultural and non-cultural factors. For instance, both groups of organizations were similar with regard to the extent of centralization, but the actions and processes which lay behind this similarity were quite different. In the English sample, there was more consultation and delegation before a final decision would be made at a senior level; whereas in the Indian sample senior managers consulted their subordinates to a lesser extent. These two different means of achieving the same end were highly consistent with the national characteristics of the English and Indian peoples.

The next chapter elaborates on this theme and proposes a multi-perspective model in which the arguments of major theories are incorporated.

PART IV
CONCLUSIONS

10
Conclusions

This book reported a cross-national study carried out in England and India in an attempt to clarify the association of cultural and social characteristics with people's work-related attitudes, and with the structure of their work organizations.

The first four chapters of the book set out the author's premises vis-à-vis the arguments advanced by the advocates of three major perspectives in the study of organizations. These are contingency, political economy, and cultural theories. The proponents of each of these attribute internal characteristics of organizations to factors in and around the organizations, such as task-environment and immediate context, national political economic institutions, and the cultural attitudes and values of organizational members respectively. The author argued that all these theories contribute to our insight into the complex issues involved in the structuring and functioning of organizations.

Chapter 5 advanced some general hypotheses about the likely links between work-related socio-cultural characteristics and aspects of organizational structures. It was argued that attitudes to power and authority, tolerance for ambiguity and uncertainty, commitment, interpersonal trust, individualism, expectations from a job, and attitudes to management practices may have significant bearing on the degree of centralization, formalization, specialization, communication pattern, control strategies and reward and punishment policies.

The empirical investigation to test these hypotheses was carried out in three stages in each of the two countries involved. The methodology employed at each stage to collect the required data was described in detail in Chapter 6. Chapters 7 to 9 discussed the findings.

The first stage of the research involved a study of socio-cultural characteristics of English and Indian peoples. It utilized available literature and the author's observations. It was accompanied by the administration of a cultural questionnaire survey conducted among an occupationally representative sample of the population in each country.

India and England were found to be different to some extent from one another in their broad socio-economic institutions, especially

Conclusions 149

their economic systems, industrial relations regulations and social stratification.

The English economy is based on a capitalistic mode of production, with a welfare state and a minimal direct government intervention in market forces. In India, the government exerts considerably more direct and indirect control over the economy.

Industrial relations legislation in India is protective of workers and aims at restricting management discretion and practices in this area to a large extent; in England the protective aspect is less marked and is currently being reduced.

Both countries are socially stratified. In England social differentiation is based on a class system which, in turn, is largely based on the amount of control and/or ownership of means of production and on profession and occupation. In India, social stratification is based on a caste system where an individual's standing in society is determined by the caste into which he is born. The English class system is far more flexible than the Indian caste structure.

The cultural surveys carried out in the two countries suggested that Indian and English peoples were different from one another in some characteristics and similar in others. The English have less fear of, and respect and obedience to, their seniors and those in position of power, they are more able to cope with ambiguity and uncertainty, more tenacious, more independent, less emotional, less fatalistic, more arrogant, more reserved and they care more for other people.

The two peoples were found to be similar with regard to honesty, tolerance, friendliness, attitudes to change, attitudes to the law, self-control and self-confidence, and acceptance of social differentiation. The cultural *attitudinal* differences were found to be consistent with the *institutionalized* differences discerned from the literature.

In the second stage of the study, a work attitude questionnaire survey was conducted among 680 employees of fourteen organizations (seven companies in each country). Both differences and similarities emerged between the two groups on the *degree* of the measures studied. English employees perceived themselves and their colleagues to have more power and autonomy at work, expressed more tolerance for ambiguity, had more positive attitudes to modern participative management practices, were less satisfied with their organization, and had different expectations from their job than did the Indian employees. To English employees both 'intrinsic' and 'extrinsic' aspects of their job were important; to Indian employees 'intrinsic' aspects were given greater significance. The difference between the two groups on their expectations from a job was evident not only in the job features that they saw as important, but also in the degree of importance they placed on these features. To Indian employees this importance was greater than to their English counterparts.

The two samples were similar with respect to trust in their colleagues, individualism, and commitment to their company. There were also similarities in the *relation* between certain work-related attitudes and some non-cultural characteristics of the respondents. For example, in both countries employees' tolerance of ambiguity decreased with the advance in age.

It was suggested that some of these differences and similarities were consistent with the employees' respective cultural backgrounds and others were not. For instance, the two samples' similar scores on trust were consistent with characteristics of their respective cultural backgrounds, but their similar scores on individualism and commitment were not. Indian employees' background is anchored in a collectivist culture and the English employees' in an individualistic one. The former was therefore expected to express a lower degree of individualism and a greater degree of commitment to their work organizations compared to the latter. This inconsistency was suggested to be explicable by non-cultural factors, such as age, hierarchical position, social status and class/caste membership.

The final stage of the research concerned a study of the same fourteen organizations. These were manufacturing firms engaged in the private sector and were matched in pairs across the two countries almost completely for industry, technology, product, size, ownership and control, status, age and markets share. The matched English and Indian organizations were found to be similar on centralization, functional specialization, chief executive's span of control, control strategies, and reward and punishment policies.

English firms were far more formalized, used job descriptions much more, and spent more time on communication and consultation, and their senior managers delegated authority further down the hierarchy.

Both cultural and non-cultural factors were found to be associated with these differences and similarities. For instance, centralization, specialization and chief executive's span of control had greater associations with task-environmental factors such as size, technology and perceived risk. Control strategies and reward and punishment policies were associated with political economic factors, such as class conflict and industrial relations. Formalization and use of job description were associated with cultural factors, such as love of privacy and independence. Communication and consultation were associated with cultural factors, such as willingness to take account of other people's opinion, and with task-contingency factors, such as market share.

Demarcation lines between various factors surrounding the organizations were also found not to be clear-cut. For instance, political economic factors, such as government industrial policies, had implications for the organizations' market share and, consequently, the competition they faced. This competition became a contingency factor for the firms.

IMPLICATIONS OF THE STUDY FOR ORGANIZATIONAL THEORY

The study provided an opportunity to examine the relevance of contingency, political economy and cultural theories for organizations. To the extent that the findings of the study can be generalized, any single explanation for organizational structure and attitudes and behaviours of their employees is rejected. These theories taken individually and in isolation from the others are found to be inadequate. The present study suggests that there is a need for a multi-perspective theory in which organization is regarded as a complex phenomenon and an outcome of complex relationships between it and various factors in and around it. These are:

Contingency theory

According to this perspective, technology and other contextual and environmental factors are determinants of organizational structure. For instance, the exponents of the 'technological implication' thesis argue that organizations with complex and unstable technologies tend to have different structural arrangements from those with simple and stable technologies. This theme is further developed in the 'culture-free' thesis, according to which the relations between organizations and their contextual factors are similar across societies.

The present study shows that, although this thesis may apply to some dimensions of organizational structure, it is inadequate for others. As was noted earlier, Indian and English organizations with similar task-environments were found to be similar on some structural aspects but not all. Also, the results of the correlation tests between structural dimensions of organizations on the one hand and their contextual variables on the other support to some extent both the contingency model and the culture-free thesis, but context–structure relationships are not all that similar between the Indian and English organizations studied here.

The pattern of relationships suggests that the universality of causal relationships applies only for those aspects of organizations which are more likely to be affected by technical and practical considerations, for example, an increase in size results in an increase in specialization. But some aspects of organizations, such as joint decisions, delegation and degree of use of written communication, are more likely to reflect employees' predispositions and the socio-cultural environments within which the organizations operate. The causal relationships among these aspects of organizations are therefore not universal. Moreover, it seems that the Western-based contingency model is more successful in predicting these relationships for English than for Indian organizations, which operate within a different sociopolitical environment, that is, one that is more similar to most eastern developing countries.

The model offered by the contingency theory is illuminating and relevant, but not sufficient.

Political economy theory

The point of this theory is that organizations operating in similar political economic systems, namely socialist or capitalist, tend to have similar characteristics, especially in terms of objectives, control strategies, and the degree of centralization of decision making. Proponents of the 'logic of industrialization' propose a 'universal' model based on the degree of industrial advancement of the countries in which the organizations operate.

The present study was conducted in two capitalist countries which have highly developed industrial sectors. However, the participating organizations, although they had similar features which were consistent with their similar capitalist industrial economic systems, were quite different from one another in many respects. This may have something to do with the level of economic development of the two countries.

Although India is an industrialized country, 75 percent of its population is still engaged in agriculture and agriculture-related occupations. The country faces enormous problems of inadequate infra-structure, poverty, illiteracy, over-population and communal tension. These problems have called for direct governmental intervention in and control of the economy which, in turn, have significant implications for Indian organizations. The present study highlighted some of these implications in areas such as market share, competition and industrial relations.

Furthermore, some of the similarities between the organizations in the two countries may not only be due to the similar political economic institutions of the two countries as industrialized nations, but also to the 200 years of British rule in India. India's industrialization and economic development, although it achieved a rapid pace after Independence in 1947, started when the British were still there and in the context of a well-established bureaucratic administration and a sophisticated civil service.

The political economy theory, although it offers valid explanations for some aspects of English and Indian organizations, does not account for those which are unique to their respective societies and may emanate from the English and Indian employees' upbringing. The cultural perspective appears to be more relevant in this respect.

Cultural theory

The present study provides some support for the arguments advanced by the culturalists, who maintain that organizational structures are determined by the socio-cultural characteristics of people inside and outside the organizations. The findings of the three stages of the study show that there was a considerable consistency between English and Indian people's socialization processes in their homes, schools, religions and societies as a whole, on the one hand, and the degree to which they held certain attitudes and values on the other. There was also some consistency between employees' cultural backgrounds and their work-related attitudes and behaviours. Finally, there was some degree of consistency between employees' work attitudes and some aspects of their organizations. The cultural theory could provide a rationale for these areas of consistency.

The study, however, also indicates that the socio-cultural characteristics of the environments within which the English and Indian organizations operated were not the only factors which affect the way they were managed and structured. Some of the hypotheses of the study which had been derived from a culturalist perspective were refuted by the present data. For instance, a lower degree of tolerance of ambiguity and uncertainty was expected to be associated with a higher degree of specialization. This was neither the case for the English organizations nor for their Indian counterparts. This dimension was closely associated with task-environmental factors.

Moreover, employees' work-related attitudes were found to be influenced not only by their cultural upbringing, but also by their age, level of education, formal position in the organizational hierarchy and the standing of their occupational group outside the organization. Also, although some work attitudes were associated more with cultural than non-cultural situational factors, there were others which had stronger relations with the situational factors. The cultural model was found useful, but it was inadequate in accounting for some of the findings of the study.

The study also exposed, and attempted to overcome, some of the methodological drawbacks of the previous cross-cultural studies. Most researchers have in the past focused their attention on the emic aspects of organizations, which are more likely to be influenced by culture, to the neglect of the etic aspects, which are inherently universal, such as technology. These researchers have incorrectly, but understandably, concluded that organizations are culture specific. The present study tried to study both these aspects of organizations.

Another drawback which many of the cross-cultural studies of management and organization still suffer from is the way they treat culture as a residual factor. The researchers simply compare, for instance, a group of managers and observe some differences in the way they view certain aspects of their work, and then, in the absence of non-cultural explanations for these differences, attribute them to culture. There is a dearth of research in which a systematic study of culture, work attitudes, and management systems is carried out in independent stages to examine the consistency between culture and management. The study reported in this book was an attempt in that direction.

The question of 'culture' versus 'nation' has not yet been clearly addressed, and many of the researchers use these concepts interchangeably. 'Culture' in its narrow sense (a set of historically evolved, learned and shared values, attitudes and meanings) seems too narrow a concept and perhaps should be replaced by 'national character'. Perhaps in future we should be concerned with the cross-national study of management. This change would reflect the view that organizations are influenced by other national institutions besides culture. The term 'nation' refers not only to culture, but also to other social, economic and political institutions which have a significant bearing on the management styles of organizations located in particular countries. The present study tried to pay attention to the implications of some national, as well as cultural, institutions, such as trade unions, government, and political economic super-structures, for business organizations.

There is also a problem of disentangling organizational culture from the societal culture which surrounds it. Hofstede (1980) tried to overcome this problem by conducting his study in subsidiaries of a multinational company. However, this meant that his study suffered from an inevitable bias, that is, American ownership and types of job. As a consequence, his samples are not representative of their respective countries. Instead, his findings map out the relative positions of different countries and occupations. In contrast, the results of the present study, which was carried out within English and Indian organizations, are to some degree representative of their respective societies. Moreover, the study exposed some of the problems with Hofstede's measurement tools, which render them inappropriate for use in most cross-national studies, certainly small-scale projects.

Present study and the multi-perspective model

Weber (1930, 1947) pioneered a multi-perspective approach when he developed the thesis that socio-cultural institutions, such as religion, had an important role in the formation of economic systems and in the degree to which organizations are administered rationally in addition to materialistic forces of the kind identified by Marx. More recently, Budde et al. (1982) compared British and West German companies and examined the role of both cultural and contingency perspectives in explaining the differences and similarities between these companies.

The multi-perspective thesis proposed here incorporates the variables suggested by contingency, political economy and cultural theories in the model shown in Figure 10.1. The model suggests that contingency factors have implications primarily for formal organizational structure, or 'etic' aspects, such as centralization and specialization. The relationships between these features of organization and contextual factors are widespread, if not universal. It is indeed common sense to expect that beyond a certain point an increase in the number of employees will lead, one way or another, to an increase in the division of labour (specialization). It is here that the universality of the organizational structures may end.

Chapter 5 argued that an understanding of organizational structure requires references not only to the formal dimensions and etic aspects, but also to the processes, relationships and actions which lie behind these dimensions. Employees' behaviours and relationships with one another within the workplace, the 'emic' aspects, are based on their work-related values and attitudes concerning such issues as power and authority, tolerance of ambiguity, commitment and management ideology and practices. These values and attitudes have strong association with the employees' cultural, occupational, educational and social backgrounds which, in turn, are rooted in their societies.

The model therefore suggests that, although in modern industrial societies business organizations tend to develop similar structural configurations in response to similar task-environments, the means by which they achieve these configurations are different, depending on the particular cultural and political economic characteristics of the society in which they operate and from which the bulk of their employees come.

156 Conclusions

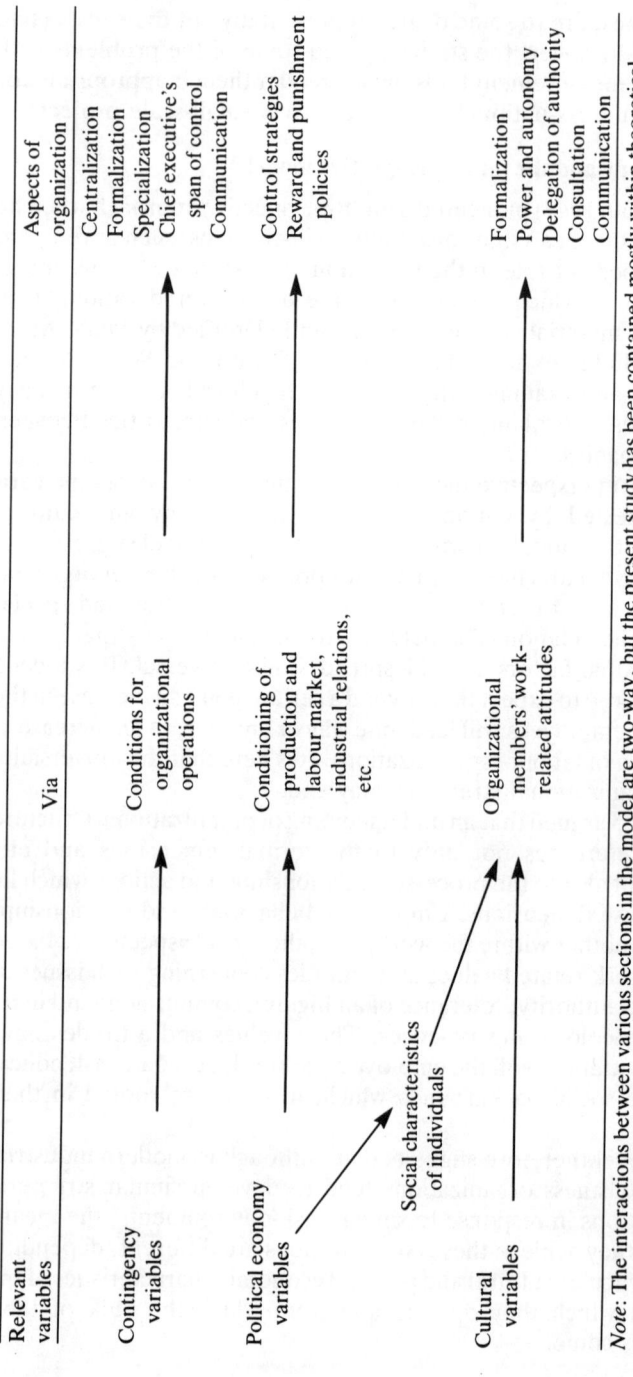

Note: The interactions between various sections in the model are two-way, but the present study has been contained mostly within theoretical perspectives in which the dominant causality is assumed to be that portrayed by the arrows shown.

Figure 10.1 *A multi-perspective model for understanding organizational structure and systems*

A reinterpretation of the findings of the studies whose authors supported a universal culture-free, or a political economy, or a culture-specific model of organizational structure in the light of the emic–etic distinction thus brings out a different conclusion. That is, all three groups may be correct in their assumptions. The first two have studied the inherently etic aspects of organizational structure and, not surprisingly, found them similar across different cultures. The third group has studied the inherently emic aspects of organizational structure and found that they varied considerably across cultures.

A more comprehensive approach to studying and understanding organizations in inter-cultural, and indeed intra-cultural, settings, such as the model suggested here, would employ a research design which enables the researchers to examine both emic and etic aspects of organizations. The conclusions thus arrived at would be more realistic than has hitherto been the case.

IMPLICATIONS OF THE STUDY FOR PRACTICE

A study such as the present one should be of value to managers and other employees in multi-cultural organizations and in developing countries. It could help to enhance understanding between employees from different cultural backgrounds. It draws the attention of managers and other designers of organizational structures to the roles that culturally-influenced traits play in influencing employees' behaviours.

The study may also assist managers to devise suitable authority structures, control strategies and inducement policies which would recognize and utilize their employees' diverse attitudes and behaviours, and which could result in a higher satisfaction for employees and a more effective management of organizations. For instance, if employees come from a culture where people generally work better under constant direction and guidance from superiors than when they are left alone with only overall objectives of the tasks at hand, then their managers could design a system which would facilitate the flow of detailed information and instruction between superiors and subordinates. Or, alternatively, these types of employees could be assigned the tasks which are routine and predictable and for which a manual of detailed instructions can be prepared.

A relevant question is how managers can measure and assess culture or, more specifically, their employees' work-related attitudes and values. Multinational corporations such as HERMES (pseudonym) (Hofstede, 1980) conduct periodical attitudinal questionnaire surveys among their employees all over the world. This kind of surveys can provide managers with information about the cultural and non-cultural characteristics of their employees. A simplified version of the work attitude questionnaire employed in the present and similar studies could be administered by a small team working in an organization's personnel department.

In the light of the complications involved in conducting attitude surveys, it might be argued that it is easier for managers and organization designers to ignore culture and instead to concentrate their attention on key, easily recognizable, contingencies. To do this might indeed be easier, but it may not necessarily be a more useful course of action, in terms of, for instance, employees' satisfaction and productivity. There is evidence that some cultural characteristics, such as attitude to power and authority relationships, can be dysfunctional (Kakar, 1971b). It has also been argued that some cultures set limits to the extent that organizations can respond and adapt to their environmental demands (Tayeb, 1979).

One way of overcoming the cultural roots of such dysfunctions may be to substitute organizational culture for national culture and change employees' attitudes and values. This is what some Japanese multinationals have tended to do. The question therefore arises as to whether culture is malleable or not.

Attitude theories suggest that people's attitudes and behaviours can be changed through communication and persuasion (Petty, 1981; Kleinke, 1984), cultural shock (Hofstede, 1978) and sustained discontinuity (Mangham, 1978). As Silverman (1970: 135) puts it, 'if the reality of the social world is socially sustained, then it follows that reality is socially changed – by action of (humans)'. Bate (1982: 27) also argues in the same vein and offers a possible way to introduce the change:

> Perhaps the initial step would be for the change agent to attempt to raise the parties' awareness of their culture – the taken-for-granted meanings that they share and collectively maintain, and which inhibit the development of effective problem solving activities.

Cross-national studies such as the present one could provide such an initial step.

Another practical implication of the present study, which was conducted in a developed country and a developing one, is that it draws the attention of the managers from developing countries to the implications for their organizations of non-technical and non-task environmental factors that are unique to their own societies. This helps them to recognize and utilize their own people's socio-cultural characteristics and devise management systems which are more authentic and appropriate to their own particular circumstances, instead of importing and applying without modifications management practices from countries with different sets of values, socio-economic conditions and political ideologies. As Kiggundu et al. (1983: 79–80) argue:

> Whenever the organization can function as a close system – either because of the nature of the practice involved or because the managers succeed in sealing its core technology from the intervention of 'outside' actors – then what we know about organization from North America seems to work fairly well. Whenever the organization interacts with its environment, however, the resulting behavior can not be understood without significant adjustments to the theories developed in industrialized nations.

Hofstede (1980: 380) compares Japan (once a developing country) and Iran (still a third-world developing country) with respect to the adoption of Western-style leadership practices and points out the dangers of ignoring culture in the process:

> Attempts at the transfer of leadership skills which do not take the values of subordinates into account have little chance of success . . . Technologies are not neutral with regard to values: in order to work, they assume that certain values are respected. Making these technologies work means that people in the receiving countries must learn new leadership and subordinateship skills, change old institutions and shift their values . . . Cultural transposition, in the ideal case, means finding a new cultural synthesis which retains from the old local values those elements deemed essential but which allows the new technologies to function. Probably the country which has most successfully done this so far is Japan; a country where it has clearly failed is Iran.

A more specific practical implication of the present research concerns Indian firms with Indian managers operating in Britain. Indian immigrants constitute a sizeable minority in this country. There are many small firms founded and managed by these people and are staffed by both English and Indian employees. The findings of the present study suggest that unless Indian managers and their English subordinates in such organizations work out suitable structures and procedures tension is to be expected in their relationships. For instance, Indian managers are likely to be reluctant to consult their subordinates and to delegate authority to them. This is incompatible with the English people's expectations, as of right, to participate and to be consulted. Indian managers are paternalistic and are likely to involve themselves in the private lives of their subordinates. This is contrary to the English people's desire and love for privacy and 'keeping themselves to themselves'.

RECOMMENDATION FOR FUTURE RESEARCH

This book has argued that a multi-perspective model is appropriate for the attempt to unravel some of the factors which may influence organizations' structures and their employees' attitudes and behaviours. The formulation advanced in the model, however, does not consider how these factors come to play their respective role in an organization *over time*. When an organization is established, the founder's cultural attitudes and values may determine and shape the organization. As the organization 'grows up', its members face shared contingencies and problems and develop shared solutions (Schein, 1984). At this stage, these shared experiences may have more influence on the way their organizations are structured and managed than do the founder's cultural traits. Here, not only the question of influence of organizational culture arises, but also the role that task environment and other contingencies play in the process. In order to understand an organization more deeply and fruitfully, it is necessary to 'dig' into its origins and the historical processes of its evolution. This clearly calls for a longitudinal cross-national case study in which the processes leading to the birth and 'growing up' of the focal organizations are reconstructed and unravelled.

A limitation of the present study was that it did not demonstrate the processes by which various cultural and non-cultural factors influence organizational structures. This issue could be addressed in future research. The research should go beyond the stage of plotting associations and non-associations between sets of variables to a more in-depth study of processes. The researcher would ideally become involved in the processes within the focal organization. The role of each set of contingency, cultural and political economic factors could then be more specifically scrutinized. An intriguing research would be one which involves an organization established by owners and managers from a different culture, such as a Japanese firm in Britain. This would allow the researcher to examine the interaction between the two different cultures and its impact on the outcome.

References

Abegglen, J.C. (1958) *The Japanese Factory*. Glencoe, Ill.: Free Press.
Adler, N.J. (1983) 'Cross-Cultural Management Research: The Ostrich and the Trend', *Academy of Management Review*, 8: 226–32.
Adorno, T.W., E. Frenkel-Brunswick, D.J. Lovinson and R.N. Stanford (1950) *The Authoritarian Personality*. New York: Harper & Row.
Aiken, M. and J. Hage (1968) 'Organizational Interdependence and Intra-Organizational Structure', *American Sociological Review*, 33: 912–30.
Aldrich, H.E. (1971) 'The Sociable Organization: A Case Study of MENSA and Some Propositions', *Social and Sociology Reviews*, 55: 429–41.
Aldrich, H.E. (1972) 'Technology and Organizational Structure: A Reexamination of the Findings of the Aston Group', *Administrative Science Quarterly*, 17: 26–43.
Aldrich, H.E. (1979) *Organizations and Environments*. Englewood Cliffs: Prentice-Hall.
Aldrich, H.E. and J. Pfeffer (1976) 'Environment of Organizations', *Annual Review of Sociology*, 2: 79–105.
Almond, G.A. and S. Verba (1963) *The Civic Culture*. Princeton: Princeton University Press.
Anderson, C.R. and F.T. Paine (1975) 'Managerial Perceptions and Strategic Behavior', *Academy of Management Journal*, 18: 811–23.
Andrews, K.R. (1960) *The Concept of Corporate Strategy*. Homwood: Irwin.
Ayoubi, Z.M. (1975) 'Technology, Size, and Structure in a Developing Country: Jordan', paper presented at the 35th Annual National Academy of Management Meetings.
Bain, G. (1983) *Industrial Relations in Britain*. Oxford: Blackwell.
Barnard, H.C. (1961) *A History of English Education From 1760*. London: University of London Press. Second ed.
Barnett, C. (1972) *The Collapse of British Power*. London: Eyre Methuen Ltd.
Barron, R.D. and G.M. Norris (1976) 'Sexual Division and the Dual Labour Market', in D.L. Barker and S. Allen (eds) *Dependence and Exploitation in Work and Marriage*. London: Longman.
Barua, S.P. (1982) *Removal of a Dead Civilization*. New Delhi: The Social Reform Movement.
Bate, P. (1982) 'Impact of Organizational Culture on Approaches to Organizational Problem-Solving', paper presented at the Conference on Qualitative Approaches to Organizations, University of Bath, 19–21 April.
Beer, S. (1982) 'The Struggle to Create a New Political Consensus', *New Society*, 16 September: 451–3.
Benedix, R. (1966) *Max Weber: An Intellectual Portrait*. London: Methuen. Paperback ed.
Benn, A.W. (1982) 'Power, Parliament and the People', *New Socialist*, September/October: 9–15.
Berlyne, D.E. (1968) 'The Motivational Significance of Collative Variables and Conflict', in R. Abelson, E. Aronson, E. McGuire, T. Newcomb, M. Rosenberg and P. Tannenbaum (eds) *Theories of Cognitive Consistency: A Sourcebook*. Chicago: Rand McNally.

162 Organizations and national culture

Beteille, A. (1969) 'Caste in a South Indian Village' in A. Beteille (ed.) *Social Inequality*. Harmondsworth: Penguin.

Blanchard, K. and S. Johnson (1982) *The One Minute Manager*. New York: Morrow.

Blau, P.M., C.M. Falbe, W. McKinley and P.K. Tracy (1976) 'Technology and Organization in Manufacturing', *Administrative Science Quarterly*, 21: 20–40.

Blau, P.M. and R.A. Schoenherr (1971) *The Structure of Organizations*. New York: Basic Books.

Bobbit, H.R. and J.D. Ford (1980) 'Decision-Maker Choice as a Determinant of Organizational Structure', *Academy of Management Review*, 5: 13–23.

Brech, E.F.L. (1953) *The Principle and Practice of Management*. London: Longman.

Brossard, M. and M. Maurice (1976) 'Is There Any Universal Model of Organization Structure?' *International Studies of Management and Organization*, 6: 11–45.

Brown, A. (1945) *Organization*. New York: Hibbert.

Buckley, W. (1967) *Sociology and Modern Systems Theory*. Englewood Cliffs: Prentice-Hall.

Budde, A., J. Child, A. Francis and A. Kieser (1982) 'Corporate Goals, Managerial Objectives, and Organizational Structure in British and West German Companies', *Organization Studies*, 3: 1–32.

Burns, T. and G.M. Stalker (1961) *The Management of Innovation*. London: Tavistock Publications.

Burrell, G. and G. Morgan (1979) *Sociological Paradigms and Organizational Analysis*. London: Heinemann.

Campbell, D. (1969) 'Variation and Selective Retention in Socio-Cultural Evolution', *General Systems*, 16: 69–85.

Caves, R.E. (1980) 'Industrial Organization, Corporate Strategy and Structure', *Journal of Economic Literature*, 18: 64–92.

Chandler, A. (1962) *Strategy and Structure*. Cambridge, Mass: MIT Press.

Chaudhuri, K.K. (1981) 'Workers' Participation in India: A Review of Studies, 1950–1980', Indian Institute of Management Calcutta working paper No. 41.

Child, J. (1972a) 'Organizational Structure, Environment and Performance: The Role of Strategic Choice', *Sociology*, 6: 1–2.

Child, J. (1972b) 'Organization Structure and Strategies of Control: A Replication of the Aston Study', *Administrative Science Quarterly*, 17: 163–77.

Child, J. (1973) 'Predicting and Understanding Organization Structure', *Administrative Science Quarterly*, 18: 168–85.

Child, J. (1980) 'Different Approaches in Comparing Capitalist and Socialist Organizations', paper presented to the Workshop on the Structure and Management of Capitalist and Socialist Organizations, Brussels, 20–22 May.

Child, J. (1981) 'Culture, Contingency and Capitalism in the Cross-National Study of Organization', in L.L. Cummings and B. M. Staw (eds) *Research in Organizational Behavior*. vol. 3. Greenwich, Conn.: JAI Press.

Child, J. (1984a) *Organization: A Guide to Problems and Practice*. London: Harper & Row.

Child, J. (1984b) 'Theoretical Perspectives in Comparing Organizations Across Social Systems', paper presented at the Third Workshop on Capitalist and Socialist Organizations, Helsinki, 29–31 August.

Child, J. and R. Mansfield (1972) 'Technology, Size and Organizational Structure', *Sociology*, 6: 369–93.

Child, J. and B. Partridge (1982) *Lost Managers: Supervisors in Industry and Society*. Cambridge: Cambridge University Press.

Child, J. and M.H. Tayeb (1983) 'Theoretical Perspectives in Cross-National Organi-

zational Research', *International Studies of Management and Organization*, 12: 23–70.
Chung, K.H. (1978) 'A Comparative Study of Managerial Characteristics of Domestic, International, and Governmental Institutions in Korea', paper presented at the Midwest Conference on Asian Affairs, Minneapolis.
Clegg, S. (1979) *Theory of Power and Organization*. London: Routledge and Kegan Paul.
Cohen, M.D., J.G. March and J.P. Olsen (1972) 'A Garbage Can Model of Organizational Choice', *Administrative Science Quarterly*, 17: 1–25.
Cook, J. and T. Wall (1980) 'New Work Attitude Measures of Trust, Organizational Commitment and Personal Need Non-Fulfilment', *Journal of Occupational Psychology*, 53: 39–52.
Crozier, M. (1964) *The Bureaucratic Phenomenon*. London: Tavistock Publications.
Crozier, M. (1973) 'The Cultural Determinants of Organizational Behavior', in A.R. Negandhi (ed.) *Modern Organizational Theory*. Kent, Ohio: Kent University Press.
Crozier, M. and J.C. Thoenig (1976) 'The Regulation of Complex Organized Systems', *Administrative Science Quarterly*, 21: 547–70.
Cummings, L.L. (1982) 'Organizational Behaviour', *Annual Review of Psychology*, 33: 541–79.
Cyert, R.M. and J.G. March (1963) *A Behavioral Theory of the Firm*. Englewood Cliffs: Prentice-Hall.
De Bettignies, H.C. (1973) 'Japanese Organizational Behaviour: A Psychological Approach' in D. Graves (ed.) *Management Research: A Cross Cultural Perspective*. Amsterdam: Elsevier Scientific Publishing.
Dill, W. (1958) 'Environment as an Influence on Managerial Autonomy', *Administrative Science Quarterly*, 2: 409–43.
Donaldson, L. (1976) 'Woodward, Technology, Organizational Structure and Performance – A Critique of the Universal Generalization', *Journal of Management Studies*, 13: 255–73.
Dore, R. (1973) *British Factory – Japanese Factory*. London: George Allen and Unwin.
Duncan, R. (1971a) 'The Effects of Perceived Environmental Uncertainty on Organizational Decision Unit Structure', unpublished doctoral dissertation, Yale University.
Duncan, R. (1971b) 'Multiple Decision Making Structures in Adapting to Environmental Uncertainty: The Impact on Organizational Effectiveness', working paper No. 54-71, Northwestern University, Graduate School of Management.
Duncan, R. (1972) 'Characteristics of Organizational Environment and Perceived Environmental Uncertainty', *Administrative Science Quarterly*, 17: 313–27.
England, G.W. and R. Lee (1971) 'Organizational Goals and Expected Behavior Among American, Japanese, and Korean Managers: A Comparative Study', *Academy of Management Journal*, 4: 425–38.
Evan, W. (1975) 'Measuring the Impact of Culture on Organizations', *International Studies of Management and Organization*, 5: 91–113.
Evers, F.T., J.M. Bohlen and R.D. Warren (1976) 'The Relationships of Selected Size and Structure Indicators in Economic Organizations', *Administrative Science Quarterly*, 21: 326–42.
Farmer, M. (1970) *The Family*. London: Longmans, Green and Co. Ltd.
Fayol, H. (1949) *General Industrial Management*. Bath: Pitman.
Ford, J.D. and J.W. Slocum (1977) 'Size, Technology, Environment, and the Structure of Organizations', *Academy of Management Review*, 2: 561–75.

Ford, J.P. (1977) 'Context, Leader Initiating Structure and Subunit Structure', unpublished manuscript, Graduate School of Business, University of Indiana. Reported in Kmetz (1978).
Friedman, A.F. (1977a) *Industry and Labour*. London: Macmillan.
Friedman, A.F. (1977b) 'Responsible Autonomy versus Direct Control over the Labour Process', *Capital & Class*, 1: 43–5.
Friedman, A.F. (1982) 'Management Strategies, Market Conditions and the Labour Process', University of Bristol discussion paper, February.
Fromm, E. (1942) *The Fear of Freedom*. London: Routledge and Kegan Paul.
Gallie, D. (1978) *In Search of the New Working Class*. London: Cambridge University Press.
Ghurye, G.S. (1932) *Caste and Race in India*. Quoted in M.N. Srinavas 'The Caste System in India' in A. Beteille (ed.) *Social Inequality*. Middlesex: Penguin.
Gore, M.S. (1965) 'The Traditional Indian Family' in N. Nimkoff (ed.) *Comparative Family System*. Boston: Houghton Mifflin.
Gorer, G. (1955) *Exploring English Character*. London: The Crosset Press.
Government of India (Ministry of Information and Broadcasting) (1982) *India 1982*. New Delhi: Research and Development Division.
Grancelli, B. (1984) 'Managerial Practices and Patterns of Employee Behaviour in Soviet Enterprise' paper presented at the Third Workshop on Capitalist and Socialist Organizations. Helsinki, August.
Grinyer, P.A. and M. Yassai-Ardekani (1980) 'Dimensions of Organizational Structure: A Critical Replication', *Academy of Management Journal*, 23: 405–21.
Hage, J. and M. Aiken (1969) 'Routine Technology, Social Structure and Organizational Goals', *Administrative Science Quarterly*, 14: 366–77.
Haire, M., E.E. Ghiselli and R.W. Porter (1966) *Managerial Thinking: An International Study*. New York: John Wiley.
Hall, R.H., J.E. Haas and N.J. Johnson (1967) 'Organizational Size, Complexity, and Formalization', *American Sociological Review*, 32: 903–12.
Hannan, M.T. and J.H. Freeman (1974) 'Environment and the Structure of Organizations: A Population Ecology Perspective', paper presented to the American Sociological Association Meetings, Montreal, Canada. August.
Haraszti, M. (1977) *A Worker in Worker's State*. Harmondsworth: Penguin.
Harbison, F. and C.A. Myers (1959) *Management in the Industrial World*. New York: McGraw-Hill.
Harbron, J. (1979) 'Korea's Executives are not Quite "The New Japanese"', *The Business Quarterly*, 44: 16–19.
Hargreaves, D.H. (1967) *Social Relations in Secondary School*. London: Routledge and Kegan Paul.
Harvey, E. (1968) 'Technology and Structure of Organizations', *American Sociological Review*, 33: 247–59.
Hedberg, B.T., P.C. Nystrom and W.H. Starbuck (1976) 'Camping on Seesaws: Prescriptions for a Self-Designing Organization', *Administrative Science Quarterly*, 21: 41–65.
Hickson, D.J., D.S. Pugh and D.C. Pheysey (1969) 'Operation Technology and Organization Structure: An Empirical Reappraisal', *Administrative Science Quarterly*, 14: 378–97.
Hickson, D.J., C.R. Hinings, C.J. McMillan and J.P. Schwitter (1974) 'The Culture-Free Context of Organization Structure; A Tri-National Comparison', *Sociology*, 8: 59–80.

Hickson, D.J., C.R. Hinings and C.J. McMillan (1981) *Organization and Nation: The Aston Programme IV*. Farnborough: Gower.

Hickson, D.J., C.J. McMillan, K. Azumi and D. Horvath (1979) 'Grounds for Comparative Organization Theory: Quick Sands or Hard Core?', in C.J. Lammers and D.J. Hickson (eds) *Organizations Alike and Unlike*. London: Routledge and Kegan Paul.

Hinings, C.R. and G.C. Lee (1971) 'Dimensions of Organization Structure and their Context: A Replication', *Sociology*, 5: 83–93.

Hiro, D. (1976) *Inside India Today*. London: Routledge and Kegan Paul.

Hirschman, A.O. (1972) *Exit, Voice and Loyalty*. Cambridge: Harvard University Press.

Hofstede, G. (1978) 'Culture and Organization; A Literature Review Study', *Journal of Enterprise Management*, 1: 127–35.

Hofstede, G. (1980) *Culture's Consequences*. California: Sage Publications.

Horvath, D., K. Azumi, D.J. Hickson and C.J. McMillan (1976) 'The Cultural Context of Organizational Control: An International Comparison', *International Studies of Management and Organization*, 1: 60–86.

Hrebiniak, L.G. and C.C. Snow (1980) 'Industry Differences in Environmental Uncertainty and Organizational Characteristics Related to Uncertainty', *Academy of Management Journal*, 23: 750–59.

Hunt, J. (1979) *Managing People at Work*. London: Pan.

Hunt, N. (1982) 'People and Politics', a series of programmes broadcast on BBC Radio World Service in August.

Inkson, J.H.K., D.S. Pugh and D.J. Hickson (1970) 'Organization Context and Structure: An Abbreviated Replication', *Administrative Science Quarterly*, 15: 318–29.

Irwin, J. (1976) *Modern Britain*. London: George Allen & Unwin.

Isamu, M. (1981) 'True Causes of Japan's Growth', *Japan Echo*, 4: 50–9.

Jacob, D. (1974) 'Dependency and Unreliability: An Exchange Approach to the Control of Organizations', *Administrative Science Quarterly*, 19: 45–59.

Jamieson, I. (1980) *Capitalism and Culture: A Comparative Analysis of British and American Manufacturing Organizations*. Farnborough: Gower.

Jelinek, M., L. Smircich and P. Hirch (1983) 'Introduction: A Code of Many Colors', *Administrative Science Quarterly*, 28: 331–8.

Jenkins, P. (1982) 'Blazing a Trail to Dignified Demise', *The Guardian*, 20 August: 15.

Kakar, S. (1971a) 'The Theme of Authority in Social Relations in India', *Journal of Social Psychology*, 84: 93–101.

Kakar, S. (1971b) 'Authority Patterns and Subordinate Behavior in Indian Organizations', *Administrative Science Quarterly*, 16: 298–307.

Key British Enterprises 1981 Compiled and published by Dun & Bradstreet Ltd., Directories Division, London.

Khandwalla, P.N. (1974) 'Mass Output Orientation of Operations Technology and Organizational Structure', *Administrative Science Quarterly*, 19: 74–97.

Kiggundu, M.N., J.J. Jorgensen and T. Hafsi (1983) 'Administrative Theory in Developing Countries: A Synthesis', *Administrative Science Quarterly*, 28: 66–84.

Kimberly, J. (1976) 'Organizational Size and the Structural Perspective: A Review, Critique and Proposal', *Administrative Science Quarterly*, 21: 571–97.

King, R. (1977) *Education*. London: Longman. Second ed.

Klein, J. (1965) *Samples from English Culture*. London: Routledge and Kegan Paul. Two volumes.

Kleinke, C.L. (1984) 'Two Models for Conceptualizing the Attitude–Behaviour Relationship', *Human Relations*, 37: 333–50.
Kmetz, J.L. (1978) 'A Critique of the Aston Studies and Results with a New Measure of Technology', *Organization and Administrative Sciences*, 8: 123–44.
Koestler, A. (1966) *The Lotus and the Robot*. London: Hutchinson. Danube edition.
Kolarska, L. and H. Aldrich (1980) 'Exit, Voice and Silence: Consumers and Managers' Response to Organizational Decline', *Organization Studies*, 1, pp. 41–58.
Kompass 1981 Compiled and published by Kompass Publishers, a Division of Information Services Limited, East Grinstead. 19th ed. (United Kingdom).
Kothari's Economic and Industrial Guide of India 1981 Compiled and published by Kothari Enterprises, Madras.
Kroeber, A.L. and C. Kluckhohn (1952) 'Culture – A Critical Review of Concepts and Definitions', papers of Peabody Museum of American Archaeology and Ethnology, Harvard University.
Kuc, B., D.J. Hickson and C.J. McMillan (1980) 'Centrally Planned Development: A Comparison of Polish Factories with Equivalents in Britain, Japan and Sweden', *Organization Studies*, 1: 253–70.
Laaksonen, O. (1948) 'The Management and Power Structure of Chinese Enterprise During and after the Cultural Revolution', *Organization Studies*, 5: 1–21.
Lammers, C.J. and D.J. Hickson (1979) *Organizations Alike and Unlike*. London: Routledge and Kegan Paul.
Lampert, N. (1984) 'Job Security and the Law in the USSR', paper presented at the Conference on Employment and Labour Policy in USSR, Birmingham, June.
Lane, D. (1977) 'Marxist Class Conflict Analyses of State Socialist Society', in R. Scase (ed.) *Industrial Society: Class Cleavage and Control*. London: George Allen and Unwin.
Lannoy, R. (1971) *The Speaking Three: a Study of Indian Culture and Society*. London: Oxford University Press.
Law, R. (1948) 'The Individual and the Community', in E. Barker (ed.) *The Character of England*. London: Oxford University Press.
Lawrence, P.R. (1975) 'Strategy: A New Conceptualization', in L.S. Sproul (ed.), *Seminars on Organizations at Stanford University*, 2: 38–40.
Lawrence, P.R. and J.W. Lorsch (1967) *Organization and Environment: Managing Differentiation and Integration*. Boston: Harvard University Press.
Littler, C.R. (1982) *The Development of Labour Process in Capitalist Societies*. London: Heinemann.
Littler, C.R. (1983) 'A Comparative Analysis of Managerial Structures and Strategies' in H.F. Gospel and C.R. Littler (eds) *Management Strategies and Industrial Relations*. London: Heinemann.
Lockett, N. and C.R. Littler (1983) 'Trends in Chinese Enterprise Management 1978–1982', *World Development*, 11: 683–704.
Lorenz, C. (1982) 'Roots of the British Malaise', *Financial Times*, 15 September: 22.
Loveridge, R. and A. Mok (1979) *Theories of Labour Market Segmentation*. Leiden: Martinus Nijhoff.
McGregor, D. (1960) *The Human Side of Enterprise*. New York: McGraw-Hill.
McKelvey, B. and H. Aldrich (1983) 'Populations, Natural Selection, and Applied Organizational Science', *Administrative Science Quarterly*, 28: 101–28.
McMillan, C.J., D.J. Hickson, C.R. Hinings and R.E. Schneck (1973) 'The Structure of Work Organizations Across Societies', *Academy of Management Journal*, 16: 555–69.
Macfarlane, A. (1978) *The Origins of English Individualism*. Oxford: Basil Blackwell.

Mackenzie, K.D. (1978) *Organizational Structure*. Arlington Heath, Ill.: AHM.
Mahoney, T. and P. Frost (1974) 'The Role of Technology in Models of Organizational Effectiveness', *Organizational Behavior and Human Performance*, 11: 122–38.
Mangham, I.L. (1978) *Interactions and Interventions in Organizations*. Chichester: Wiley.
Mansfield, R. (1973) 'Bureaucracy and Centralization: An Examination of Organizational Structure', *Administrative Science Quarterly*, 18: 477–88.
Marsh, R.M. and H. Mannari (1976) *Modernization and the Japanese Factory*. Princeton: Princeton University Press.
Marsh, R.M. and H. Mannari (1981) 'Technology and Size as Determinants of the Organizational Structure of Japanese Factories', *Administrative Science Quarterly*, 26: 33–57.
Martin, D. (1967) *A Sociology of English Religion*. London: Heinemann.
Maslow, A.H. (1954) *Motivation and Personality*. New York: Harper and Row.
Maurice, M. (1976) 'Introduction: Theoretical and Ideological Aspects of the Universalistic Approach to the Study of Organizations', *International Studies of Management and Organization*, 6: 3–10.
Maurice, M., A. Sorge and M. Warner (1980) 'Societal Differences in Organizing Manufacturing Units: A Comparison of France, West Germany and Great Britain', *Organization Studies*, 1: 59–86.
Mayhew, B.H., R.L. Levinger, J.M. McPherson and T.F. James (1972) 'System Size and Structural Differentiation in Formal Organizations; A Baseline Generator for Two Major Theoretical Propositions', *American Sociological Review*, 37: 629–33.
Mayo, E. (1945) *The Social Problems of an Industrial Civilization*. Boston: Harvard University Press.
Meade, R.D. (1967) 'An Experimental Study of Leadership in India', *Journal of Social Psychology*, 72: 35–43.
Mehta, V.R. (1982) ' "Centre and Periphery" in Indian Politics', *Government and Opposition*, 17: 164–79.
Meyer, M.W. (1979) 'Organizational Structure as Signalling', *Pacific Sociological Review*, 22: 481–500.
Miles, R.E. and C.C. Snow (1978) *Organizational Strategy, Structure, and Process*. New York: McGraw-Hill.
Miller, D., M.F. Kets de Vries and J.M. Toulouse (1982) 'Top Executive Locus of Control and its Relationship to Strategy-Making, Structure, and Environment', *Academy of Management Journal*, 25: 237–53.
Mintzberg, H. (1979) *The Structuring of Organizations*. Englewood Cliffs: Prentice-Hall.
Mitchell, T.R. (1985) 'In Search of Excellence versus the Best 100 Companies to Work for in America: A Question of Perspective and Values', *Academy of Management Review*, 10: 350–5.
Mohr, L.B. (1971) 'Organizational Technology and Organizational Structure', *Administrative Science Quarterly*, 16: 444–59.
Mooney, J. (1947) *Principles of Organization*. New York: Harper and Row.
Naisbitt, J. (1982) *Megatrends*. New York: Warner.
Nam, W.S. (1971) 'The Traditional Pattern of Korean Industrial Management', ILCORK working paper No. 14, Social Science Research Institute, University of Hawaii.
Negandhi, A.R. (1985) 'Management in the Third World', in P. Joynt and M. Warner (eds) *Managing in Different Cultures*. Oslo: Universitetsforlaget.

Negandhi, A.R. and S.B. Prasad (1971) *Comparative Management.* New York: Merdith Corporation.
Osborn, R. and J. Hunt (1974) 'Environment and Organization Effectiveness', *Administrative Science Quarterly*, 19: 231–64.
Ouchi, W. (1981) *Theory Z: How American Business Can Meet the Japanese Challenge.* Reading, Mass.: Addison-Wesley.
Parekh, B. (1974) 'The spectre of Self-Consciousness', in B. Parekh (ed.) *Colour, Culture, and Consciousness.* London: George Allen and Unwin.
Pascale, R.T. (1978) 'Zen and the Art of Management', *Harvard Business Review*, 56: 153–62.
Pascale, R.T. and A.G. Athos (1982) *The Art of Japanese Management.* London: Penguin.
Pascale, R.T. and M.A. Maguire (1980) 'Comparison of Selected Work Factors in Japan and the United States', *Human Relations*, 33: 433–55.
Pennings, J.M. (1973) 'Measures of Organizational Structure: A Methodological Note', *American Journal of Sociology*, 79: 686–704.
Pennings, J.M. (1975) 'The Relevance of the Structural-Contingency Model for Organizational Effectiveness', *Administrative Science Quarterly*, 30: 393–410.
Perrow, C. (1967) 'A Framework for the Comparative Analysis of Complex Organizations', *American Sociological Review*, 32: 194–208.
Perrow, C. (1970) *Organizational Analysis: A Sociological View.* Belmont, CA: Wadsworth.
Perrow, C. (1977) 'The Types of Effectiveness Studies', in P.S. Goodman, J.M. Pennings and Associates (eds) *New Perspective on Organizational Effectiveness.* London: Jossey-Bass.
Peters, T.J. and R.H. Waterman (1982) *In Search of Excellence: Lessons from America's Best Run Companies.* New York: Harper & Row.
Petty, R.E. (1981) 'The Role of Cognitive Responses in Attitude Change Processes', in R.E. Petty, T.M. Ostrom and T.C. Brock (eds) *Cognitive Responses in Persuasion.* Hillsdale, NJ: Erlbaum.
Pfeffer, J. (1972) 'Merger as a Response to Organizational Interdependence', *Administrative Science Quarterly*, 17: 218–28.
Pfeffer, J. and G.R. Salancik (1974) 'Organizational Decision Making as a Political Process: The Case of a University Budget', *Administrative Science Quarterly*, 19: 135–51.
Pfeffer, J. and G.R. Salancik (1978) *External Control of Organizations: A Resource Dependence Perspective.* New York: Harper & Row.
Pietsch, A-J. (1984) 'Shortage of Labour and Motivation Problems of Soviet Workers', paper presented at the Conference on Employment and Labour Policy in USSR, Birmingham, June.
Piore, J.M. (1972) 'Notes for a Theory of Labor Market Stratification', working paper no. 95, Department of Economics, MIT.
Popper, K.R. (1979) *Objective Knowledge: An Evolutionary Approach.* Oxford: Clarendon Press (rev. ed.).
Pugh, D.S., D.J. Hickson, C.R. Hinings and C. Turner (1968) 'Dimensions of Organization Structure', *Administrative Science Quarterly*, 13: 65–105.
Radke, M. (1946) 'The Relation of Parental Authority to Children's Behavior and Attitudes', University of Minnessota monograph on child welfare, 22.
Ramu, G.N. (1981) 'Research in the Family in India', *Indian Journal of Social Research*, XXII: 58–65.

Ray, C.A. (1986) 'Corporate Culture; The Last Frontier of Control?', *Journal of Management Studies*, 23: 287–97.
Raynor, J. (1969) *The Middle Class*. London: Longmans, Green & Co. Ltd.
Reeves, T.K. and J. Woodward (1970) 'The Study of Managerial Control', in J. Woodward (ed.) *Industrial Organization: Behaviour and Control*. London: Oxford University Press.
Reid, I. (1977) *Social Class Differences in Britain*. London: Open Books.
Reimann, B.C. and G. Inzerilli (1979) 'A Comparative Analysis of Empirical Research on Technology and Structure', *Journal of Management*, 5: 167–92.
Roberts, K. (1978) *The Working Class*. New York: Longman.
Roberts, K.H. (1970) 'On Looking at an Elephant: An Evaluation of Cross-Cultural Research Related to Organizations', *Psychological Bulletin*, 74: 327–50.
Roderick, G. and M.D. Stephenson (1978) *Education and Industry in the Nineteenth Century: The English Disease*. London: Longman.
Roderick, G. and M.D. Stephenson (1981) *Where Did We Go Wrong?: Industry, Education and Economy of Victorian Britain*. London: The Falmer Press.
Roderick, G. and M.D. Stephenson (1982) *The British Malaise; Industrial Performance, Education and Training in Britain Today*. London: The Falmer Press.
Roethlisberger, F.G. (1944) *Management and Morale*. Cambridge, Mass.: Harvard University Press.
Rokeach, M. (1979) *Understanding Human Values: Individual and Societal*. New York: The Free Press.
Rose, G. (1968) *The Working Class*. London: Longman.
Rowntree, B.S. and G.R. Lavers (1951) *English Life and Leisure: A Social Study*. London: Longmans, Green and Co.
Rumelt, R.P. (1986) *Strategy, Structure and Economic Performance*. Boston, Mass.: Harvard Business School (rev. ed.).
Sampson, A. (1982a) *The Changing Anatomy of Britain*. London: Hodder & Stoughton.
Sampson, A. (1982b) 'Who Runs Britain'. A series on BBC Television, October.
Schein, E.H. (1984) 'Coming to a New Awareness of Organizational Culture', *Sloan Management Review*, Winter: 3–16.
Schoonhoven, C.B. (1981) 'Problems with Contingency Theory: Testing Assumptions Hidden within the Language of Contingency "Theory"', *Administrative Science Quarterly*, 20: 349–77.
Scott, B. (1970) *Stages of Corporate Development*. Boston, Mass.: Harvard Business School.
Scott, W.R. (1975) 'Organizational Structure', *Annual Review of Sociology*, 1: 1–20.
Segal, R. (1971) *The Crisis of India*. Bombay: Jaico Publishing House.
Shenoy, S. (1981) 'Organization Structure and Context: A Replication of the Aston Study in India', in D.J. Hickson and C.J. McMillan (eds) *Organization and Nation*. Farnborough: Gower.
Silverman, D. (1970) *The Theory of Organizations*. London: Heinemann.
Smircich, L. (1983) 'Concepts of Culture and Organizational Analysis', *Administrative Science Quarterly*, 28: 339–58.
Smith, P.B. (1984) 'The Effectiveness of Japanese Styles of Management: A Review and Critique', *Journal of Occupational Psychology*, 57: 121–36.
Smith, P.B. and M.F. Peterson (1988) *Leadership in Context: A Cultural Analysis of Organizational Behaviour*. London: Sage Publications (in press).
Smith, P.B. and M.H. Tayeb (1988) 'Organizational Structure and Processes', in M.

Bond (ed.) *The Cross-Cultural Challenge to Social Psychology*. California: Sage Publications (in press).

Soeters, J.L. (1986) 'Excellent Companies as Social Movements', *Journal of Management Studies*, 23: 300–12.

Sorge, A. (1983) 'Cultural Organization', *International Studies of Management and Organization*, 12: 106–38.

Sorge, A. and M. Warner (1980) 'The Societal and Organizational Context of Industrial Relations: A Comparison of Great Britain and West Germany', *Industrial Relations Journal*, 11: 41–9.

Sorge, A. and M. Warner (1981) 'Culture, Management and Manufacturing Organizations: A Study of British and German Firms', *Management International Review*, 21: 35–48.

Spender, J-C. (1980) 'Strategy-Making in Business', unpublished PhD thesis, Manchester Business School.

Sugarman, B.N. (1966) 'Social Class and Values as Related to Achievement Conduct in School', *Sociological Review*, 14: 289–301.

Tannenbaum, R. and W.H. Schmidt (1958) 'How to Choose a Leadership Pattern', *Harvard Business Review*, 36: 95–101.

Tayeb, M.H. (1979) 'Cultural Determinants of Organizational Response to Environmental Demands', unpublished M.Litt. thesis, University of Oxford.

Tayeb, M.H. (1984) 'Nations and Organizations: A Comparative Study of English and Indian Work-Related Attitudes and Values in Manufacturing Firms', PhD thesis, Aston University.

Taylor, F.W. (1911) *Scientific Management*. New York: Harper and Row.

Terry, P. (1979) 'An Investigation of Some Cultural Determinants of English Organization Behaviour', unpublished PhD thesis, University of Bath.

Thompson, J.D. (1967) *Organizations in Action*. New York: McGraw-Hill.

Thompson, J.D. and F.L. Bates (1957) 'Technology, Organization, and Administration', *Administrative Science Quarterly*, 2: 325–43.

Thorelli, H. (1967) 'Organizational Theory: An Ecological View', proceedings of the Academy of Management: 66–84.

Times of India Directory and Yearbook 1980–1981 Compiled and published by The Times of India Press, Bombay.

Triandis, H.C. (1981) 'Dimensions of Cultural Variations as Parameters of Organizational Theories', paper presented at the International Symposium on Cross-cultural Management, Montreal, Canada. October.

Trist, E. (1981) 'The Evolution of Socio-Technical Systems; A Conceptual Framework and an Action Research Programme', issued in the Quality of Working Life Centre, a series of occasional papers, No. 2, June.

Tushman, M.L. (1978) 'Technological Communication in R & D Laboratories: The Impact of Project Work Characteristics', *Academy of Management Journal*, 22: 624–45.

Urwick, L.F. (1943) *The Elements of Administration*. New York: Harper.

Van de Ven, A.H. and A. Delbecq (1974) 'A Task-Contingent Model of Work-Unit Structure', *Administrative Science Quarterly*, 19: 183–97.

Van de Ven, A.H., A. Delbecq, D. Emmet and S. Mendenhall (1974) 'A Structural Examination of the Unit Design', unpublished paper, Kent University, Kent, Ohio.

Watson, T.J. (1980) *Sociology, Work and Industry*. London: Routledge and Kegan Paul.

Weber, M. (1930) *The Protestant Ethic and the Spirit of Capitalism*. London: George Allen & Unwin.

References 171

Weber, M. (1947) *The Theory of Social and Economic Organization*. New York: Free Press.
Weber, M. (1961) *General Economic History*. New York: Collier Books.
Weick, K.E. (1969) *The Social Psychology of Organizing*. Reading, Mass.: Addison-Wesley.
Weick, K.E. (1976) 'Educational Organizations as Loosely Coupled Systems', *Administrative Science Quarterly*, 21: 1–20.
White, P.E. (1974) 'Resources as Determinants of Organizational Behavior' *Administrative Science Quarterly*, 19: 366–79.
Wiener, M.J. (1981) *English Culture and the Decline of the Industrial Spirit: 1850–1980*. London: Cambridge University Press.
Woodward, J. (1958) *Management and Technology*. London: HMSO.
Woodward, J. (1965) *Industrial Organizations: Theory and Practice*. London: Oxford University Press.
Woodward, J. (1970) *Industrial Organizations: Behaviour and Control*. London: Oxford University Press.
Yassai-Ardekani, M. (1979) 'A Multivariate Analysis of Structure, Context, Strategy and Style', unpublished PhD thesis, City University Business School.
Zwerman, W.L. (1970) *New Perspective in Organization Theory*. Westport, Conn.: Greenwood.

Index

Abbreviated Aston Schedule, 70–1
Abegglen, J.C., 35
action, bias for, 24, 26
actions, 43
Adler, N.J., 3
administrative intensity, 9
Adorno, T.W., 45
age
 role, 3, 67–8, 70, 146
 work-related attitudes and, 134, 136, 137, 138
aggregate environment, 15
agriculture (India), 15
Aiken, M., 12, 71
Aldrich, H.E., 14, 17, 20, 30
All India Radio, 84
Almond, G.A., 99
Alpha coefficient, 58, 59, 60, 121, 122, 124
ambiguity, tolerance of, 39, 44–5, 48, 74, 116–19, 135–6
'analysers', 19
Anderson, C.R., 17
Andrews, K.R., 19
'Archive of the National Study', 20, 22, 69
arranged marriages, 76
Aston Programme, 20, 22, 114, 115
 Abbreviated Schedule, 70–1
 formalization scale, 141
Athos, A.G., 36
attitudes
 about others, 128, 129
 toward control system, 128, 129
 toward law, 99–100
 toward participation, 128, 129
 work-related, *see* work-related attitudes
authority, 3, 4, 27, 44, 96–7
 concentration, *see* centralization; decentralization

delegation, 47, 71, 114, 127, 132, 145, 146, 147
 -power relationship, 44, 109–15, 134–5
 see also control; power
autonomy, 25, 46–7
 perceived, 71, 115
 responsible, 31–2, 139
Ayoubi, Z.M., 14

Bain, G., 86
Barnard, H.C., 80
Barnett, C., 78
Barron, R.D., 31
Barua, S.P., 97
Bate, P., 158
Bates, F.L., 11
BBC (government influence), 83
Beer, S., 82
Bendix, R., 77
Benn, A.W., 82
Berlyne, D.E., 45
Beteille, A., 79
Bharatya Janata Party, 84
bias for action, 24, 26
Blanchard, K., 24
Blau, P.M., 12, 14
Bobbit, H.R., 17
Brech, E.F.L., 9
bribery, 99
Britain, 30, 37–8, 41
 see also England
Brossard, M., 20, 37
Brown, A., 9
Buckley, W., 17
Budde, A., 155
Buddhists, 78
bureaucracy, 9–10, 15
Burns, T., 15–16
Burrell, G., 2
Business Weekly, 25–6

174 Index

Calvinism, 77
Campbell, D., 17
capitalism, 28–31, 32, 33, 77, 78, 85, 141
career systems, 2
   see also occupation
caste system, 55, 78–9, 87, 94, 98, 136–7
Caves, R.E., 41
censorship (media), 83, 84
central workers, 31–2
centralization, 1, 30, 144
   organizational structure and, 3, 9, 16, 20, 43, 70–1, 132, 139–40, 147
   power distance, 38–9, 44, 48, 114–15
'centrally noted backward areas', 86
Chandler, A., 19
character/characteristics
   comparisons, 101–3
   English, 77, 88–90, 148–9
   Indian, 91–3, 148–9
Chauduri, K.K., 87
chief executive (span of control), 19–20, 70, 71, 145
Child, J., 7, 28
   contingency theory, 22–3
   cultural theory, 34, 35–6, 40
   National Study, 20, 22, 69
   organizational structure, 1, 4–5, 9, 10, 13, 14, 27, 141, 144
   personal flexibility scale, 116, 118
   strategic choice, 4, 17, 18
child-rearing, 74–5, 76–7, 103
China, 30–1
Christianity, 77–8
Chung, K.H., 37
Church of England, 77
classical theory, 10, 22
Clegg, S., 9
co-ordination, 2
'coalignment', 23
coefficients
   Alpha, 58–60, 121, 122, 124
   K-R8, 58, 116–18, 121–2, 124
Cohen, M.D., 16
collectivism, 29, 39, 97
   group-orientation, 3, 45–6, 120
commercial capitalism, 85
commitment, 44, 45–7, 48, 120–3, 136–7
communication, 23, 47, 141, 144–7
   patterns, 70, 71–2, 128, 130, 131, 132
Communist Party of India, 84

community consciousness, 95, 97
competition, 18, 70
complexity, 9
configuration, 2, 20
Congress Party (India), 84
'congruence', 23
conservatism, English, 101
Conservative Party, 82–3, 85, 86, 141
consultation, 2, 43, 44, 48, 128, 130, 141, 147
'consults' leadership style, 60–1
context-structure relations, 1, 7, 10, 141–7, 151
contextual factors, 1–3, 5, 7, 10, 23, 50, 51
   culture-free thesis, 3, 21–2, 24, 54, 115, 151, 157
   organizational structure survey, 68–9, 108–9
   see also environment
contingency theory, 2, 4–5, 6
   Aston Programme, 20, 22, 114, 115
   context-structure, 7, 10, 141–7, 151
   contextual factors, 50, 51
   culture-free thesis, 3, 21–2, 24, 54, 115, 151, 157
   environment, 15–18
   implications of study, 151–2
   industry, 18–19
   overall view, 22–4
   size, 14–15
   strategy, 19–20
   technology, 11–14, 144–5
control
   chief executive's, 19–20, 70, 71, 145
   direct, 31–2, 47, 139
   ownership and, 144, 146
   strategies, 31–2, 123–4, 132–3, 139
   systems, 70, 72, 122–3, 128, 129
   systems (influences), 44, 45, 47–8
   see also authority; formalization; power
Cook, J., 45, 47, 121, 123–4
core items
   power distance index, 60–1, 63
   uncertainty avoidance index, 63–4
corporate development, 19
correlation tests, 57–60, 63, 134, 144
corruption, 4, 99
Council of Ministers/States, 83

Index

coupling, 1, 16
cross-cultural study (problems), 1–3, 6, 154–5
cross-national study (background), 1–7
Crozier, M., 4, 36–7
cultural survey, 148–9
  research design/methodology, 49–56
  results, 88–93
  settings, 73–106
cultural theory, 2, 4–5, 7
  implications of study, 153–5
  Iranian study, 5–6
  overall view, 40–1
  studies, 34–40
cultural values/attitudes
  comparisons, 101–3
  England, 94–101
  India, 94–101
culture
  cross-cultural study (problems), 1–3, 6, 154–5
  definitions and scope, 42–3
  -free thesis, 3, 21–2, 24, 54, 115, 151, 157
  national, 27, 39, 154
  organization and (hypothetical model), 42–8
  organizational structure and, 107–33
  work-related attitudes, 130–2
  see also non-cultural factors
Cummings, L.L., 9
Cyert, R.M., 17

De Bettignies, H.C., 28, 34
decentralization, 6, 10, 14, 15, 18, 23, 27, 30, 38–9
decision-making, 24
  centralized, *see* centralization
  consultation, 2, 43, 44, 48, 128, 130, 141, 147
  decentralized, 6, 10, 14, 15, 18, 23, 27, 30, 38–9
  decision units, 16–17
  delegation, 47, 71, 114, 127, 132, 145, 146, 147
  hypothetical model, 43–8
  joint decisions, 71, 114, 132, 146
'defenders', 19
deference (to seniors), 96–7
Delbecq, A., 12

delegation, 47, 71, 114, 127, 132, 145, 146, 147
democracy, 82–4
dependence, 13, 20, 100–1, 103
design strategy, 49–50, 51
differentiation (functional), 37–8
Dill, W., 15
direct control, 31–2, 47, 139
discipline
  family, 74–5, 76–7
  self-control and, 94–5
division of labour, *see* specialization
'dominant coalition', 17
dominant technology, 70
Donaldson, L., 12
Doordarshan (television network), 84
Dore, R., 27–8, 32, 85
dual hierarchies, 30
dual labour market, 31–2, 36
Duncan, R., 16

economic structures, 6–7, 23, 30–1
  supra-structures, 27, 32, 33
economic systems, 28–31, 85–6
education
  England, 79–80
  India, 81
  role, 3, 65–7
  work-related attitudes and, 134, 135, 136, 137, 138
élitism, 17, 39, 80, 81, 94
emic aspects, 26, 43, 154, 155, 157
employees (samples), 107–8
England, 41
  characteristics, 77, 88–90, 148–9
  cultural survey, 52–4
  cultural values/attitudes, 94–101
  cultural values (comparison), 101–3
  location and population, 73
  organizational structure survey, 68–72, 159
  organizations (study of), 107–33
  social institutions, 74–90
  work-related attitudes survey, 56–61, 63–8, 103–6, 149–50
England, G.W., 37
entrepreneurship, 25
environment, 4–5, 23
  task, 1, 15, 37, 41, 148, 158
  uncertainty, 10, 13, 15–19

Index

environmental determinism, 17
etic aspects, 26, 43, 154, 155, 157
Evan, W., 40
Evers, F.T., 14
excellence, theory of, 24–6
executives (behaviour), 19–20
Exit, Voice and Loyalty (Hirschman), 30
expertise, 7, 9, 43
export policies, 20, 23
'extrinsic' job factors, 149

factor analysis, 57, 58–62
fair play, 95–6
family life
  England, 74–5
  India, 75–7
Farmer, M., 74
fatalism, 79, 101
Fayol, H., 9
femininity, 39
feudalism, 77
Financial Times, 84, 85, 86
fiscal policy, 85
focal organization, 15, 20
Ford, J.D., 9, 13, 17
Ford, J.P., 20
formalization, 9, 16, 20, 39
  structure and, 43, 45, 48, 70, 71, 119, 132, 141, 145
France, 36–8
free will, 79
Freeman, J.H., 17
Friedman, A.F., 13, 27, 31
Fromm, E., 45
Frost, P., 12
functional differentiation, 37–8
functional integration, 37–8
functional specialization, 70, 71, 145, 146

Gallie, D., 33, 37–8, 86
'garbage can' model, 16
Gentleman, The, 79
Germany, 37
Ghurye, G.S., 55
global interdependence, 3
goal-setting/attainment, 15
Gore, M.S., 54
Gorer, G., 41, 53, 74, 77, 100

government
  England, 82, 83
  India, 55, 83–4
Grancelli, B., 29
Grinyer, P.A., 14, 20
group-orientation, 3, 45–6, 120
group morality, 97
Guardian, The, 86

Hage, J., 12, 71
Haire, M., 21, 128, 129, 134
Hall, R.H., 14
Hannan, M.T., 17
Haraszti, M., 29
Harbison, F., 27, 32
Harbron, J., 37
Hargreaves, D.H., 80
Harvard Business School, 19
Harvey, E., 12
Hedberg, B.T., 1, 16
height (production hierarchy), 70, 71
HERMES, 63, 157
Hickson, D.J., 1, 13, 14, 20, 21
hierarchies, 30–1, 35, 37, 39, 43, 65
  production, 70, 71
Hinduism, 54, 78–9
Hinings, C.R., 14, 22
Hiro, D., 54
Hirschman, A.O., 30
Hofstede, G., 4, 38–41, 44, 46, 58, 63–8, 116–17, 134, 154, 157–9
honesty, 99
Horvath, D., 20
House of Commons/Lords, 82
House of People, 83
Hrebiniak, L.G., 18
human relations school, 10, 22, 28
Hunt, J., 9, 14, 15
Hunt, N., 82

ideational approach, 7, 34, 50
ideological supra-structures, 33
imports, 85, 86, 141
In Search of Excellence (Peters and Waterman), 24–5
independence, 46, 100, 101, 103
India
  characteristics, 91–3, 148–9
  cultural survey, 52–6

cultural values, 94–101
location and population, 73
organizational structure survey, 68–72, 159
organizations (study of), 107–33
social institutions, 75–94
work-related attitudes survey, 56–60, 62–8, 103–6, 149–50
India Today, 85, 86, 95, 97, 99
India Express, 81, 99
individualism, 32, 39, 44, 46, 78, 80, 97, 120–1, 137
industrial capitalism, 85
industrial relations, 6, 65, 87, 140
Industrial Revolution, 32–3, 74, 78, 86
industrialization, logic of, 27–8, 32, 152
industry variable, 18–19, 69–70
information
  censorship, 83, 84
  sharing, 43, 128, 129, 138
ingroup, 46
Inkson, J.H.K., 14, 70, 119
institutional approach, 34, 50
integration (functional), 37–8
internal reliability test, 57–60, 121, 123
internationalism, 3
interpersonal trust, 43, 47, 123–4
interview schedule/scales, 69–72
intra-organization structural variations, 16
'intrinsic' job factors, 149
Inzerilli, G., 13
Iranian study, 5–6, 44, 56, 58, 63, 127, 158
Irwin, J., 86
Isamu, M., 36

Jacob, D., 18
Jains, 78
Jamieson, I., 33, 38, 97
Janata Party, 55, 84
Japan, 27–8, 30, 34–6
Jelinek, M., 3
Jenkins, P., 80
job-description, 119
job definition, 45
job expectations, 46, 124–8, 137–8
job security, 35–6, 137, 138
Johnson, S., 24
'joins' leadership style, 60

joint decisions, 71, 114, 132, 146
joint family, 75–6

K-R8 coefficient, 58, 116–18, 121–2, 124
Kakar, S., 37, 54, 96, 97, 130, 158
Karala, 107
Karnataka, 107
Key British Enterprises, 69
Khandwalla, P.N., 12, 13, 20, 23
Kiggundu, M.N., 159
Kimberley, J., 15
King, R., 80
kinship system, 78
Klein, J., 74
Kleinke, C.L., 158
Kluckhohn, C., 42
Kmetz, J.L., 20
Koestler, A., 54, 95
Kolarska, L., 30
Kompass 1981, 69
Kothari's Economic and Industrial Guide of India, 69
Kroeber, A.L., 42
Kuc, B., 30

Laaksonen, O., 30
labour, 87
  employees (samples), 107–8
  market, 31–2, 36
  turnover, 31, 35, 38
  see also working class
Labour Party, 82–3, 85, 86
Lammers, C.J., 1
Lampert, N., 29
Lane, D., 28
Lannoy, R., 54, 75
late development syndrome, 28
Lavers, G.R., 77, 99
Law, R., 95
law (attitudes toward), 99–100
Lawrence, P.R., 10, 16, 23
leadership style, 60–1, 63, 159
Lee, G.C., 14, 22
Lee, R., 37
Liberal Party, 82–3, 85, 86
lifetime employment, 35–6
'linkages', 146
Littler, C.R., 30, 36
Lockett, N., 30
logic of industrialization, 27–8, 32, 152

Index

Lok Dal, 84
Lok Sabha, 83
loosely coupled systems, 1, 16
Lorenz, C., 80
Lorsh, J.W., 10, 16, 23
Loveridge, R., 36
Luther, Martin, 77

Macfarlane, A., 32, 74, 78, 85
McGregor, D., 10
McKelvey, B., 17
Mackenzie, K.D., 9
McMillan, C.J., 20
macro environment, 15
Maguire, M.A., 36
Maharashtra, 54–5, 68, 107
Mahoney, T., 12
management, 31
   control, *see* control
   leadership style, 60–1, 63, 159
   mechanistic, 11, 15
   organic, 11, 15–16
   participative, 21, 27, 128, 129
   practices, 27–8, 128–30, 138–9, 146, 158–9
   strategic choice, 4, 17, 18
managerial prerogatives, 30, 38
Mangham, I.L., 158
Mann-Whitney test, 114, 119, 127
Mannari, H., 11, 12, 13, 14, 36, 145
Mansfield, R., 13, 14, 20
manual workers, 53–4, 56
March, J.G., 17
market mechanisms, 23, 29–32
market share, 18, 70, 141, 145, 146
marriage relationships, 74, 75, 76
Marsh, R.M., 11, 12, 13, 14, 36, 145
Martin, D., 77
Marx, Karl, 155
masculinity, 39
Maslow, A.H., 124, 127
mass media, 83, 84–5
matching, 4, 10, 49
Maurice, M., 1, 2, 20, 22, 37, 115
Mayhew, B., 14
Mayo, E., 10
Meade, R.D., 130
mechanistic management, 11, 15
media, 83, 84–5
Megatrends (Naisbitt), 24

Mehta, V.R., 86, 94
methodology, 49–72, 154
Meyer, M.W., 9
'middle castes', 94
middle class
   England, 53–4, 74–5, 80, 87, 136
   India, 94
Miles, R.E., 19
Miller, D., 19
Mintzberg, H., 42
Mitchell, T.R., 25
mixed economy (India), 85–6
Mohr, L.B., 12
Mok, A., 36
monetarism, 85
Mooney, J., 9
Morgan, G., 2
motivation, 29, 45, 46–7, 120
multi-cultural societies, 3
multi-perspective model, 2, 7, 151, 155–7, 160
multinational corporations, 3, 37–8, 40, 63, 157–8
multiple power centres, 30
Muslims, 78
Myers, C.A., 27, 32

Naisbitt, J., 24
Nam, W.S., 37
national culture, 27, 39, 154
'natural selection' model, 17
need hierarchy, 124, 127
needs (and abilities), 10
Negandhi, A.R., 1
neo-liberalism, 82
neo-radicalism, 82
neo-socialism, 82
newspapers, 83, 84–5
nomothetic cross-national design, 49
non-cultural factors, 1, 3
   organizational structure and, 139–47
   power distance and, 64–7
   uncertainty avoidance and, 67–8
   work-related attitudes and, 134–9
non-manual workers, 53–4, 56
Norris, G.M., 31

objectives (organizational), 28–9
observations, 52

occupation
  class differentiation and, 53, 55–6
  role, 3, 64–7
  status, 31, 35, 65, 66–7
  work-related attitudes, 134–5, 137–8
Official Secrets Act, 83
oligopolistic firms, 35–6
'one best way', 9–10, 22
One Minute Manager (Blanchard and Johnson), 24
'open door' policies, 18, 141
optimum performance, 10–11
organic management, 11, 15–16
organizational
  analysis (problems), 1–3
  culture, 40, 158
  élitism, 17, 39, 80, 81
  strategy, 19–20
  theory, 24, 151–7
  variables, 50, 51
organizational structure
  context-structure, 1, 7, 10, 141–7, 151
  contingency theory, 2, 11–24
  cross-national study, 4–7
  cultural theory, 2, 34–41
  culture and (hypothetical model), 42–8
  non-cultural factors, 139–47
  political economy theory, 2, 27–33
  survey, 50, 68–72
  universal theories, 9–26
  work-related attitudes hypotheses, 103–6
  work-related attitudes survey, 107–33
organizations (study of)
  discussion, 132–3
  results, 109–30, 150–1
  samples, 108–9
  universal theories, 9–26
Osborn, R., 14, 15
Ouchi, W., 2, 24, 28, 34
outgroup, 46
ownership, 70, 144, 146

Paine, F.T., 17
parallelism (authority structures), 4
Parekh, B., 54, 94–5, 97, 99, 119
parliamentary democracy, 82–4
participative management, 21, 27
  attitudes toward, 128, 129

Partridge, B., 116, 118
party hierarchy, 30
party systems, 82–4
Pascale, R.T., 36
Pearson correlation test, 59, 60, 63, 134, 144
Pennings, J.M., 15, 20
People's Party, 84
perceived autonomy, 71, 115
perceived boss, 61, 63
perceived power, 109, 111, 112–15, 139
perceived risk, 140
perceived uncertainty, 16
performance criteria, 11–13
performance levels, 10–11, 19, 127–8
peripheral workers, 31–2
Perrow, C., 11, 12, 13, 23
personal flexibility scale, 116, 118
Peters, T.J., 24–5, 26
Peterson, M.F., 26
Petty, R.E., 158
Pfeffer, J., 17, 18
Pietsch, A-J., 29
Piore, J.M., 31
Poland, 30
political-economic factors, 50, 51
political contingency, 23
political economy, 2, 6, 7
  implications of study, 152–3
  labour market and management control strategies, 31–2
  logic of industrialization, 27–8, 32, 152
  overall view, 32–3
  socio-economic system, 28–31
political systems, 82–5
Popper, K.R., 12
population ecology model, 17
power, 37
  -authority relationship, 43, 44, 109–15, 134–5
power distance, 38–9, 44, 48, 139
  index, 60–1, 63
  non-cultural factors, 64–7, 68
  work-related attitudes survey, 58–67, 111–12
Prasad, S.B., 1
preferred boss, 61, 63, 112
pressure groups, 83
primary sector, 31

primary social institutions, 74–94
problem-solving approach, 74
processes, 43
product, 70
production hierarchy, 70, 71
production technology, 12, 23, 70
production units, 70
productivity, 13, 24, 25, 29
profit/profitability, 13, 29, 31
promotion, 35
property rights, 28
'prospectors', 19
protectionism, 5, 85–6, 141
Protestant ethic, 32, 77, 101
Protestantism, 77–8
public school system, 80, 81
Pugh, D.S., 9, 20, 22, 43
punishment, 70, 72, 127–8, 138, 140
Puri, Rajinder, 84

qualifications, 2, 138
questionnaires, 52–3, 56–8, 148, 149
questions (validation), 58–68

Radke, M., 74
Rajya Sabha, 83
Ramu, G.N., 75
Ray, C.A., 25
Raynor, J., 74, 94, 98
'reactors', 19
Reeves, T.K., 12
regional culture, 39
Reid, I., 54
Reimann, B.C., 13
relationships, 43, 44, 109–15, 134–5
religions, 54, 77–9
research
    design strategy, 49–50, 51
    future recommendations, 160
    implications, 151–9
    methodology (cultural survey), 49, 50, 52–6
    methodology (organizational structure survey), 50, 68–72
    methodology (work-related attitudes survey), 50, 56–68
    problems, 1–3, 49
research and development, 70, 140
resource dependence model, 17–18

resourcefulness, 98–9
responsibility (acceptance), 100–1
responsible autonomy, 31–2, 139
reward, 70, 72, 127–8, 138, 140
risk, 19, 39, 43, 44–5, 140
Roberts, K., 2, 75
Roderick, G., 78
Roethlisberger, F.G., 10
Rokeach, M., 134
Rose, G., 75
Rowntree, B.S., 77, 99
rule orientation, 63, 67, 68
rules, 27, 39, 45
Rumelt, R.P., 19
rural areas, 54
rural élite, 94

Salancik, G.R., 18
samples (cultural survey), 107–9
sampling procedures, 25, 50, 53–6, 72
sampling size, 56, 72
Sampson, A., 80
Schmidt, W.H., 60
Schoenherr, R.A., 14
school systems, 80, 81
Schoonhoven, C.B., 22, 144
Scott, B., 9, 19
secondary sector, 31
secondary social institutions, 74–94
Segal, R., 54, 76, 83, 84, 97, 99, 101
selectivity rules, 9
self-control, 94–5
self-orientation, 46
'sells' leadership style, 60
sexual discrimination, 42–3
shared management, 37
Sharma (on *Financial Times*), 84
Shenoy, S., 132
Sikhs, 78
Silverman, D., 158
simple-complex dimension, 16
size, 13, 14–15, 23, 38, 70, 145, 146
skill categories, 54
Slocum, J.W., 9, 13
Smircich, L., 3
Smith, P.B., 26, 28, 35
Snow, C.C., 18, 19
social class, 98
    England, 53–4, 87
    India, 55–6, 87, 94

Social Democratic Party, 82
social élite, 80
social institutions, 74–94
social organizations, 17
social settings (organizations)
  cultural values, 94–101
  discussion, 101–3
  institutions, 74–94
  work-related attitudes hypotheses, 103–6
social structures, 6–7
socialism, 28–31, 33, 82, 84
socialization process, 39, 42, 101, 153
societal effect approach, 37
socio-economic structure
  England, 85, 86–90
  India, 85–6, 87, 91–4
socio-economic system, 28–31
Soeters, J.L., 24, 25
Sorge, A., 7, 37
South Korea, 37
specialization, 10, 20, 27, 39, 43, 48, 119, 132, 140
  functional, 70, 71, 145, 146
Spender, J.C., 18
stage model (development), 19
Stalker, G.M., 15–16
standardization, 20, 39, 48
Statesman, The, 84
static-dynamic dimension, 16
status
  occupational, 31, 35, 65, 66–7
  organizations, 20, 69, 70, 145–6
Stephenson, M.D., 78
strategic choice, 4, 17, 18
strategy, 19–20
stress, 63, 67, 68
structural dimensions, 114
  context-structure relations, 1, 7, 10, 141–7, 151
sub-castes, 55, 78–9, 94
sub-units, 16
Sugarman, B.N., 80
Sunday Observer, 84
surveys
  cultural, 50, 52–6
  organizational structure, 50, 68–72
  work-related attitudes, 50, 56–68
Sweden, 30

Tannenbaum, R., 60
task environment, 1, 15, 37, 41, 148, 155
Tayeb, M.H., 1, 7, 13, 23, 26, 28, 34–6, 72, 134
  Iranian study, 5–6, 44, 56, 58, 63, 127, 158
Taylor, F.W., 9
technological change, 144, 145
technological imperative, 12–13, 27
technological implications thesis, 151
technological requirements, 31, 32
technology-structure fit, 12–14, 23
Telegraph, The, 97
'tells' leadership style, 60
Teresa, Mother (of Calcutta), 95
Terry, P., 41, 53, 95, 98, 100, 119
textbooks, 81
Thatcher, Margaret, 82
Theory Z (Ouchi), 24
Thoenig, J.C., 36–7
Thompson, J.D., 11, 14, 17, 23
Thorelli, H., 15
Times, The, 86–7, 95
Times of India, 69, 81
tolerance of ambiguity, 39, 44–5, 48, 74, 116–19, 135–6
tolerance of others' opinions, 96
trade unions, 6, 33, 38, 82
  England, 86–7
  India, 87, 101
training, 10, 21, 31
Triandis, H.C., 46
Trist, E., 13
trust, 44, 48, 137
  honesty and, 99
  interpersonal, 43, 47, 123–4
Tushman, M.L., 23

uncertainty avoidance
  index, 58–64, 67–8
  tolerance of ambiguity, 39, 44–5, 48, 74, 116–19, 135–6
United States, 34–6, 38
universal theories, 152
  contingency, 9–22
  contingency (overall view), 22–4
  excellence, 24–6
universalism, 21, 22
'Untouchables', 55, 79

Index

urban areas (India), 54
Urwick, L.F., 9

Van de Ven, A.H., 12
Varimax rotated factor matrix, 59–62
Verba, S., 99

wages, 31, 137–8, 140
Wall, T., 45, 47, 121, 123–4
Warner, M., 37
Waterman, R.H., 24–5, 26
Watson, T.J., 31
Weber, M., 9, 32, 77, 85, 155
Weick, K.E., 1, 16, 17
White, P.E., 18
Wiener, M.J., 78, 80, 97
Woodward, J., 11, 12, 23
work-related attitudes
 culture and, 130–2
 hypotheses, 103–6
 non-cultural factors, 134–9
 organizational structure and, 132–3
 survey, 50, 56–68, 149–50
 survey, organizational structure and, 107–33
work ethic, 32, 77, 101
work structuring, 2
worker participation, 87
working class, 28, 29
 England, 53–4, 75, 80, 87, 136
working conditions, 31
works committees, 87
'world views', 2

Y theories, 28
Yasai-Ardekani, M., 14, 20, 139

Z organizations, 24
Zoroastrians, 78, 95
Zwerman, W.L., 12